The Tobacco Wars

Walter Adams

and

James W. Brock

 South-Western College Publishing
an International Thomson Publishing company I(T)P®

Cincinnati • Albany • Boston • Detroit • Johannesburg • London • Madrid • Melbourne • Mexico City
New York • Pacific Grove • San Francisco • Scottsdale • Singapore • Tokyo • Toronto

Publishing Team Director:	Jack W. Calhoun
Acquisitions Editor:	Keri Witman
Production Editor:	Mardell Toomey
Production House:	DPS Associates, Inc.
Cover Design:	Jennifer L. Martin
Marketing Manager:	Lisa L. Lysne

2 3 4 5 6 7 8 9 WL 6 5 4 3 2 1 0 9

Printed in Canada

I(T)P®
International Thomson Publishing
South-Western College Publishing is an ITP Company.
The ITP trademark is used under license.

To Col. J.E.B.
WWII gunner, bombardier, pilot, missileman
Legion of Merit

"For thy sake, Tobacco,

I would do anything but die."

— Charles Lamb,
A Farewell to Tobacco, 1830

"Tobacco is a filthy weed,

That from the devil does proceed;

It drains your purse, it burns your clothes,

And makes a chimney of your nose."

— Benjamin Waterhouse

Table of Contents

Preface

As a general proposition, one might say (to paraphrase James Baldwin) that the anguish that often overtakes an industry tends to come late in its life. It's a time when it must make the almost inconceivable effort to divest itself of everything it has ever expected or believed, when it must take itself apart and put itself together again, walking out of the world into limbo or into what certainly looks like limbo.

Today, the multibillion-dollar tobacco industry finds itself in that position. It is the focus of a fierce national debate—second, perhaps, only to controversies over gun control, affirmative action, and abortion.

The industry is accused of killing 400,000 Americans every year—more than AIDS, alcohol, car accidents, murders, suicides, and illegal drugs combined! Critics call smoking "history's deadliest man-made epidemic."

On the legal front, some 40 states have sued the tobacco giants, charging them with operating an illegal cartel to suppress price competition and to stifle research and development in the search for a "safe" cigarette. Scores of counties, cities, and health organizations have joined in this parade of litigation.

In Washington, Congress and the White House have engaged in a bitter, multipartisan struggle to fashion legislation to deal with the industry—especially the problem of youth smoking.

Aficionados of the theater of the absurd[1] would find the character of the debate intimately familiar. There is an absence of communication—a terrifying diversity of utterances, with the

---

[1] See Martin Esslin, *The Theater of the Absurd* (New York: Anchor Books, 1961). For specimens of the genre, see plays by Samuel Becket, Arthur Adamov, Eugene Ionesco, and Vaclav Havel. For a pioneering venture by an economist as playwright, see Leonard Silk, *Veblen: A Play in Three Acts* (New York: A.M. Kelley Publishers, 1966).

actors on stage listening only to snatches and fragments of the dialogue, and responding as if they had not listened at all. At times the dialogue consists of statements that are in and of themselves perfectly lucid and logically constructed but lacking in context and relevance. At other times, absurd ideas are proclaimed as if they were axiomatic truths. In this dialogue of the deaf, advocacy takes precedence over consensus.

Above all, there is a degradation of language—a recourse to verbal banality. In an age of mass communication, language has run riot. Words border on the meaningless and lack authentic content. Does the correlation between smoking and lung cancer, emphysema, and heart disease *prove* that cigarettes are the *cause* of these maladies? Is smoking a free consumer choice, a *habit* like drinking coffee, watching television, or eating gummy bears; or is it an *addiction* that makes the very notion of free choice ridiculous? To resolve such issues requires more than ossified clichés, empty formulas, and popular slogans.

Why did we write this book? Why this choice of genre? Primarily to put the tobacco controversy in perspective. Primarily to lay bare the states of mind and images that constitute the hidden assumptions in the debate—to provide an intersection between what is visible and what is under the surface, to expose the latent content that forms the essence of the controversy, and to expose the disguised meaning of the words used by the protagonists in the debate. Our dialogue finds absurdity not in the depths of the irrational, but in what on the surface appears to be the very essence of rationality. It seeks to demonstrate that "a false vocabulary systematically places the debate on false ground and makes it practically impossible to analyze the concrete reality."[2]

The setting for our "play" is a five-part public affairs television series in which representatives of the pro- and antitobacco forces debate the central issues of the current tobacco wars. Our purpose

---

[2] Milan Kundera, "Candide Had to Be Destroyed," in Jan Vladislav, ed., *Vaclav Havel, or Living in Truth* (London: Faber and Faber, 1986), 261.

is to make the audience think about these issues analytically and dispassionately. Our hope is that people will take this form of television theater seriously and that, in turn, this form of theater can perform a serious educational function.

Walter Adams
James W. Brock

I. The Antecedents

MODERATOR: Good evening, and welcome to the first program in our five-week series, *The Tobacco Wars.*

Next to debates over affirmative action and abortion, smoking is one of the most fiercely debated issues in American public policy:

- Public health researchers blame tobacco for killing 400,000 Americans every year—more than die from AIDS, alcohol, car accidents, murders, suicides, illegal drugs, and fires combined[1]—and call smoking "history's deadliest man-made epidemic."[2]
- The Office of Technology Assessment claims that smoking is responsible for some $70 billion in health care costs annually.[3]
- According to a Florida court, "No cocaine cartel, gambling empire, or white-collar scheme has even approached the damage allegedly done" by the tobacco industry.[4]
- Recent decades have seen an explosion of No Smoking bans—in restaurants, on commercial airline flights, in offices and workplaces, and even in bars and taverns.
- Television and radio advertising of tobacco products has been banned, while cigarette packs and other forms of advertising must prominently feature government-ordered statements detailing the hazards of smoking.

THE TOBACCO WARS

Tobacco is the basis for a multibillion-dollar industry that is dominated by a few large firms. Cigarettes account for over 90 percent of spending on tobacco products in the United States, and last year American consumers smoked about 24 billion packs. Smokeless tobacco, cigars, and pipe tobacco are also produced by the tobacco industry. In 1995, U.S. spending for all tobacco products totaled about $49 billion.

Five American companies—Philip Morris, R. J. Reynolds (a subsidiary of RJR Nabisco), Brown and Williamson (a subsidiary of B.A.T. Industries), Lorillard (a subsidiary of Loews), and Liggett—produce almost all of the cigarettes sold in the United States. Two companies, Philip Morris and R. J. Reynolds, account for more than 70 percent of industry sales. About 36 billion packs of cigarettes were produced by U.S. firms in 1997, with about 12 billion packs exported to other countries and about 280 million packs shipped to U.S. territories and to U.S. armed forces stationed overseas. The rest were consumed by domestic smokers. Cigarette revenues totaled about $46 billion in 1996.

Smokeless tobacco products are also produced by only five domestic manufacturers: U.S. Tobacco, Conwood, Pinkerton, National, and Swisher. Over 120 million pounds of chewing tobacco and snuff were produced in the United States in 1996; in 1995, smokeless tobacco companies posted revenues of $1.7 billion. Cigars and pipe tobacco are produced in a market that is less concentrated in a few companies. About 2.5 billion large cigars and cigarillos and 14.2 million pounds of pipe and roll-your-own tobacco were produced by U.S. companies in 1995.

The United States is the second largest tobacco producer in the world, falling well below China in total production. In 1996, tobacco was grown on over 124,000 U.S. farms, producing a crop valued at $2.9 billion. The Department of Agriculture administers a system of marketing quotas, which supports the price of tobacco, as well as a loan program for tobacco producers. The quota system has no significant costs other than those of administration. Over time, the loan program is intended to pay for itself.

The tobacco industry supports over 600,000 jobs for people who produce and deliver tobacco products. In addition, 625,000 retail outlets distributed cigarettes and tobacco products in 1992. Convenience stores and gas stations sold about $12.7 billion in tobacco products that year, with vending machines adding $2 billion in sales.

Source: Congressional Budget Office, *The Proposed Tobacco Settlement: Issues from a Federal Perspective,* (Washington, DC: GPO April 1998).

- Despite 30 years of warnings, ad bans, and ever more restrictive prohibitions, however, public health officials report an alarming upsurge in the number of young smokers. "Joe Camel" ads have been blamed—and banished—for contributing to this trend.
- On the legal front, numerous states have sued the tobacco companies, charging them with operating an illegal cartel to eliminate competition and demanding compensation for the health expenses that the states say they've incurred to treat smoking-related sicknesses.
- In Washington, a proposed mega-billion dollar settlement between states and the industry has sparked political infighting in the Senate and the House as Congress and the president wrestle with the economics and politics of tobacco policy.

Tonight, to provide an overview for our series, we are joined by two distinguished guests: Our first panelist is one of the nation's leading economic historians. She has published numerous articles on the industry, and her latest book is considered the definitive history of tobacco. Professor, welcome and thank you for being with us.

HISTORIAN: Thank you. It's a pleasure to join you.

MODERATOR: Also with us tonight is the former chief executive of one of the world's largest tobacco companies, a person who literally grew up in the business, and who in his retirement continues to follow events in the field. Welcome, sir.

EXECUTIVE: Thank you for inviting me.

MODERATOR: Professor, let's begin with you. In your recent book you write, "The tobacco industry is unique in the persistence and passion of the controversies it has engendered." Would you explain the basis for that statement?

HISTORIAN: Certainly. Every grade school child learns that Columbus arrived in the New World in 1492, and that he and other voyagers found this new world a remarkable place.

From the very beginning, smoking was an issue.

Of all the astonishing things they encountered, however, one of the most frightening and intriguing was the natives' custom of breathing smoke! From Brazil to Canada, the early discoverers encountered indigenous peoples who cultivated and consumed dried tobacco leaves. In fact, some native tribes called their smoking implements "tobocas"—from whence the word "tobacco" is derived. And there seemed no limit to the variety of ways they consumed their tobacco: smoking, chewing, drinking, licking, snuffing —even tobacco enemas.[5] Some tribes even tracked time in terms of pipefuls of tobacco consumed.

MODERATOR: Yet you write that the tobacco wars commenced from the very outset. Why?

HISTORIAN: Those early explorers, including the priests who accompanied them, believed the smoke exhaled by these fire-breathing creatures to be evidence not only of savagery but, more alarming, of possession by the Devil! They exhorted their troops to resist the evil weed, and tried strenuously to dissuade them from smoking it. One cleric warned: "As the devil is a deceiver and knows the virtues of herbs, he showed them the value of this plant so that they might see imaginary things and fantasies which it reveals to them, and thus he deceives them."[6]

Alas, such warnings were futile because, as Columbus himself observed, once his troops experimented with tobacco, "It was not within their power to refrain from indulging in the habit."[7]

MODERATOR: And that irresistible attraction accompanied the transfer of tobacco back to Europe?

HISTORIAN: It certainly did: Tobacco joined coffee, cane sugar, peanuts, and maize as an immensely popular gift from the New World.

MODERATOR: Controversy also accompanied tobacco's trip back?

HISTORIAN: Absolutely. Legend has it that when one of Columbus's scouts returned to Spain and lit up the first cigar, terrified townspeople ran immediately to the local priest! The first non-Indian smoker had clashed with the first antismoking group—in this case, the Spanish Inquisition—and the fellow was thrown in prison.[8]

Curiously, it was what Europeans believed to be the medicinal benefits of tobacco that greatly enhanced its early appeal. A 1577 work entitled *Joyfull Newes of our Newe Founde Worlde,* for example, glowingly described the virtues of tobacco for curing "griefs of the head," "griefs of the stomach," "griefs of the Joints," "venemous Carbuncles," "old Sores," "worms," and "cuttings, strokes, pricks, or any other manner of wound." It also reported the plant's mysterious power for allaying hunger and thirst as well as removing the weariness of labor.[9]

Intrigued by its mystical healing virtues, a French ambassador to the Portuguese court, Jean Nicot—from whose name the term *nicotine* is derived—smuggled tobacco seeds back to France. Once cultivated, the leaves of those seeds were pulverized and presented to the king's mother to sniff as a cure for her chronic headaches!

Some clerics also began to revise their initial spiritual condemnations of smoking. Some of them began to reason that "smoking expelled the humors from the brain and body, with the result that smokers were less liable than others to the temptations of the flesh."[10]

Regardless, tobacco consumption spread like wildfire throughout Europe and most of the rest of the world. Within two generations, smoking was generally considered a panacea for almost every ailment—preventing the plague, serving as laxative and disinfectant, warding off depression, even enhancing memory!

MODERATOR: So far it all sounds positive enough. Why did the controversy persist?

EXECUTIVE: Since I too have studied this aspect of tobacco's history, may I respond to your question?

MODERATOR: Certainly, please do.

EXECUTIVE: I believe the controversy continued because smoking, like anything new, is always viewed suspiciously by the powers that be: Christian religious leaders denounced it as a pagan act of heresy, while in the Middle East and Orient smoking was condemned as a subversive Christian trick. Popes threatened to excommunicate smokers, while Russian czars banished them to Siberia. The lips of Hindustan smokers were cut; Chinese tobacco traffickers were executed; and Persian smokers were condemned to having molten lead poured down their throats![11]

As I point out to my antismoking friends today, they're neither original nor very imaginative.

HISTORIAN: In fact, some four hundred years ago, in his 1604 *Counter-Blaste to Tobacco,* England's James I articulated what would become the classic case against smoking. He deplored it as "a custom loathsome to the eye, hateful to the nose, harmful to the brain, dangerous to the lung, and the black stinking fume thereof, nearest resembling the horribly Stygian smoke of the pit that is bottomless"—and he raised tobacco import duties by 4,000 percent in order to discourage its consumption![12]

MODERATOR: With all those condemnations and ghastly punishments, how was it that tobacco consumption flourished?

EXECUTIVE: I think for two reasons: First, and most obviously, people enjoyed it immensely. . . .

MODERATOR: The focus of next week's program. . . .

EXECUTIVE: And the second reason for the great expansion of tobacco consumption, ~~I believe, was that governments found it to be an incredibly lucrative business—to conduct and, especially, to tax~~. The Spanish government might have imprisoned smokers early on, but by the mid-1700s the Royal Tobacco Factory at Seville had become Spain's largest employer.[13] Although he railed against tobacco consumption, James I was astute enough to declare it a British royal monopoly in order to capture the profits thrown off by a product that sold, at times, at a price equal to its weight in silver. Even the Vatican eventually launched its own tobacco factory.[14]

~~By the time of the American Revolution, tobacco accounted for three-quarters of all goods exported from Virginia and Maryland; in fact, Ben Franklin was able to borrow foreign funds to finance the Revolution by pledging Virginia leaf tobacco as collateral.~~[15]

~~Today, 50 million Americans spend approximately $50 billion annually on tobacco products~~. Tobacco also is one of the few American export success stories: U.S. tobacco exports exceed imports by a factor of 20![16]

MODERATOR: What about tobacco as a source of tax revenue today?

EXECUTIVE: Tobacco is one of the most heavily taxed of all commodities: ~~By 1875, taxes on tobacco accounted for one-third of all government revenue in the United States.~~[17] Today, federal and state taxes average over 50¢ a pack and generate some $13 billion in annual tax receipts.[18]

MODERATOR: Is there any variation among the states in their taxation of tobacco?

EXECUTIVE: Quite a bit—as you can see on Graphic 1-1.

MODERATOR: Hasn't there been an explosion of cigarette tax hikes in recent years?

EXECUTIVE: Yes, indeed. ~~Since February 1997, at least ten states have increased their cigarette tax levies.~~ The following amounts give you some indication of the trend:

- Alaska from 29¢ to $1, effective October 1, 1997
- Hawaii from 60¢ to 80¢, effective September 1, 1997
- Illinois from 44¢ to 58¢, effective December 15, 1997
- Maine from 37¢ to 74¢, effective November 1, 1997
- New Hampshire from 25¢ to 37¢, effective July 1, 1997
- New Jersey from 40¢ to 80¢, effective January 1, 1998
- Oregon from 28¢ to 68¢, effective February 1, 1997
- Rhode Island from 61¢ to 71¢, effective July 1, 1997
- Utah from 26.5¢ to 51.5¢, effective July 1, 1997
- Wisconsin from 44¢ to 59¢, effective November 1, 1997[19]

GRAPHIC 1-1

STATE CIGARETTE TAX RATES PER PACK OF 20 CIGARETTES; 1998

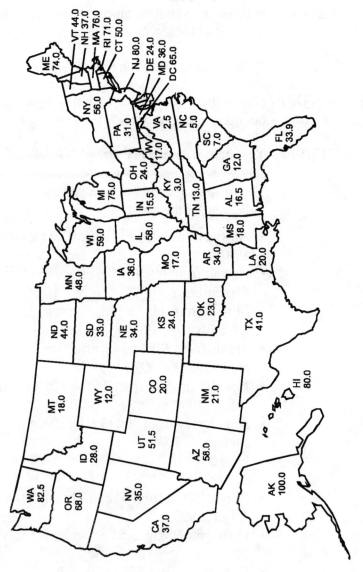

Source: U.S. General Accounting Office, *Tobacco: Issues Surrounding a National Tobacco Settlement* (Washington, DC: GPO, April 1988), p. 16.

Other states may soon join the parade.

MODERATOR: On the federal level, hasn't President Clinton recently proposed raising tobacco taxes as a painless way to generate $60 billion to fund a host of government childcare, education, and crime programs?[20]

EXECUTIVE: Not painless for smokers, of course. It's all part of the administration's tax and spend program.

MODERATOR: Well, tax policy is another topic we'll explore at greater length in upcoming programs. So let's move on with our general overview.

HISTORIAN: An interesting sidelight is that the particular ways in which people chose to consume tobacco in the 16th and 17th centuries came to be differentiated by socioeconomic class: Aristocrats preferred to imbibe their tobacco through ostentatious displays of snuff taken in fancy parlor rooms; the working classes and rebellious youths smoked their tobacco in the streets and coffee houses.[21] In fact, in postrevolutionary France cigarettes became a popular symbol of antiroyalist protest![22]

Also, personal hygiene in those days was, shall we say, undeveloped. As a result, smoking was considered one way to mask a rather pungent kind of air pollution.[23]

MODERATOR: Professor, in your book you write that the tobacco wars in America took on a new dimension at the beginning of the 20th century.

HISTORIAN: That's right. Concerns about monopolization of the industry by James Duke and his American Tobacco Trust replaced fantasies about fire-breathing devils.

MODERATOR: And while these monopoly issues will be the focus of our third program, why don't you give us a brief overview of this aspect of the tobacco wars.

HISTORIAN: Certainly. In 1890, at the height of the trust and consolidation movement in American industry, James Duke engineered a merger combining the nation's five leading cigarette firms. The result of that combination, the American Tobacco Company, controlled 90 percent of the nation's entire cigarette business.[24]

EXECUTIVE: Madam, you know that in those days cigarettes accounted for only a small portion of the tobacco trade. Plug, snuff, chew—that's where the big volume was.

HISTORIAN: I agree. Apparently so did Mr. Duke, because his acquisitive drive didn't stop at cigarettes. Employing a variety of predatory tactics, he exploited the profits from his cigarette monopoly to force producers of other tobacco goods either to merge with his firm or to abandon the field. By 1910, his American Tobacco Company had acquired some 250 formerly independent firms and operations. He controlled 86 percent of national cigarette output, 85 percent of plug production, 76 percent of smoking tobacco, 80 percent of fine-cut tobacco, 97 percent of snuff, and 91 percent of little cigars.[25]

EXECUTIVE: I reject your characterization! The fact is that Mr. Duke *earned* his position through old-fashioned American entrepreneurship: superior goods, advanced methods of mass production, brilliant distribution and marketing campaigns!

HISTORIAN: Not according to the Supreme Court, which in 1911 found American Tobacco guilty of violating the nation's antitrust statutes, and ordered the firm dismembered into 14 independent and separate companies, including Lorillard, Liggett & Myers, R. J. Reynolds, and a vastly reduced American Tobacco Company.[26]

MODERATOR: And did that antitrust action successfully reestablish competition in the industry?

EXECUTIVE: Yes!

HISTORIAN: No! What the Justice Department and the Court did was replace a monopoly with a tight oligopoly—an industry dominated by a few large firms—in this case the Big Four firms carved from the old tobacco trust. As a result, 30 years later the Justice Department launched another antitrust lawsuit against the industry—another case in which yet another Supreme Court convicted the largest firms of collectively monopolizing the field.[27]

EXECUTIVE: A travesty of justice: We were convicted for behaving as sensible businesspeople.

MODERATOR: Be assured that all aspects of these antitrust issues will be examined thoroughly in our third program.

Overall, then, issues of competition and monopoly joined health issues in fanning the tobacco wars?

HISTORIAN: Yes, and they've continued to do so down to the present. Individual states are now suing the tobacco companies for colluding to eliminate competition in researching health problems, conspiring to prevent competition in disseminating accurate health information to consumers, and avoiding competition in developing less hazardous tobacco products.

Joining the states in a growing parade of litigation are large cities—notably San Francisco, Los Angeles, and New York—as well as labor unions, health insurance firms, and even asbestos companies![28]

EXECUTIVE: I hope your viewers appreciate just how bizarre my industry's situation has become: On the one hand, we're attacked for encouraging too many people to smoke; on the other hand, we're condemned for not competing vigorously enough to encourage *more* people to smoke!

HISTORIAN: That's not quite a fair characterization. It's a question of restraining competition to research the health consequences of smoking; restraining competition to better inform people about those dangers; restraining competition to develop less hazardous products from which consumers can choose.

EXECUTIVE: Well, I must say it's a peculiar notion of competition that requires an industry to dissuade people from freely choosing to consume its products!

MODERATOR: I think we see some difference of opinion on this issue, which, to repeat, we'll explore in greater depth two weeks from tonight.

But to return to our historical overview, would it be correct to say that in more recent decades health concerns have returned to the forefront of the tobacco wars?

EXECUTIVE: That's like saying a little ice interrupted the Titanic's voyage!

HISTORIAN: Actually, the health concerns never disappeared. Early in this century, cigarettes quickly came to dominate all other forms of American tobacco consumption. In an effort to arrest this development, the "crusading schoolmarm," Lucy Page Gaston, launched her National Anti-Cigarette League, and actually ran for president in the 1920 election.

EXECUTIVE: It should be noted that Miss Gaston—who never consumed a bit of tobacco in her entire life—perished from throat cancer shortly after her presidential campaign.

HISTORIAN: But the fact is that as long ago as 1893, a number of states had outlawed the manufacture, sale, use or advertising of cigarettes; in 1907, Illinois outlawed all four![29]

EXECUTIVE: On the other hand, I remember that when asked what it would take for America to win

World War I, General "Black Jack" Pershing shot back, "Tobacco as much as bullets"—a request to which the YMCA and the Red Cross responded with alacrity. In World War II, cigarettes were even used in place of currency in prisoner of war camps.[30]

HISTORIAN: Yet Thomas Edison refused to employ smokers. And Henry Ford warned: "If you study the history of almost any criminal, you will find he is an inveterate smoker." Cigarettes, Ford believed, seduced American youth into lives of depravity in billiard rooms and saloons.[31] An elementary school textbook of that era warned students that tobacco poisoned the "cells of the brain" and, as a result, smokers' "ideas may lack clearness of outline," and the "ability to seize and hold an abstract thought may be impaired." "If a father finds that his boy is fibbing to him, is difficult to manage, or does not wish to work," warned one counselor, "he will generally find that the boy is smoking cigarettes."[32]

EXECUTIVE: Nevertheless, the states subsequently recognized the folly of their prohibitionist ways and repealed their laws banning tobacco. Thereafter, the number of Americans voluntarily choosing to smoke cigarettes— and I emphasize the words *voluntarily choosing*—grew enormously. Graphic 1-2 shows that cigarette sales increased from a rate of 54 cigarettes per capita in 1900 to 4,300 cigarettes per capita by 1963.[33] There's simply no denying that people greatly enjoyed smoking.

GRAPHIC 1-2

ADULT PER CAPITA CIGARETTE SALES AND MAJOR
SMOKING-AND-HEALTH EVENTS

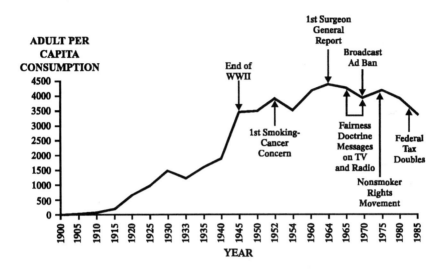

Source: U.S. Department of Health and Human Services, Public Health Service, Office on Smoking and Health, *Reducing the Health Consequences of Smoking: 25 Years of Progress*, (Washington, DC: GPO, 1989), p. 659.

HISTORIAN: I don't dispute your facts. Nonetheless, concerns about the health threats of smoking also grew in importance, especially beginning in the early 1950s when Dr. Ernst Wynder, a young epidemiologist, published the results of his pathbreaking experiments finding that a disproportionate number of mice developed cancerous tumors after their shaved backs were painted with distilled cigarette tar.[34]

EXECUTIVE: I recall asking Dr. Wynder at the time if he had ascertained just how many humans made

it a practice to distill cigarette tar and paint it
on their backs!

Besides, a person would have to smoke
something like 64 cartons of cigarettes a day
for 75 years in order to absorb an amount of
tar and nicotine equivalent to that which the
good doctor inflicted on his poor mice.

HISTORIAN: You may ridicule his results, but a number of
highly influential groups took his findings and

those reported by a number of other
researchers quite seriously.[35] The American
Medical Association, for example, responded
by halting cigarette advertisements in its
journals and publications.[36]

EXECUTIVE: Madam, I assure you our industry took those
findings very seriously as well. In 1954, 14
leading tobacco firms joined together to form
the Tobacco Industry Research Council, or
TIRC, as a collaborative effort for examining
the health issues in a responsible manner. In
full-page ads purchased in hundreds of
newspapers across the country, we declared
our "interest in people's health as a basic
responsibility, paramount to every other
consideration in our business."[37]

HISTORIAN: Others dispute your characterization of the
TIRC. They charge it was a propaganda tool
for minimizing, distorting, and ignoring the
health concerns being raised about smoking.
It was essentially created by the public
relations firm Hill & Knowlton—and even
held its meetings just one floor below Hill &
Knowlton's offices! Even employees of the

organization and its successor describe it as "just a lobbying thing."[38] The companies viewed their collective research endeavor as the "best and cheapest insurance the tobacco industry can buy and without it, the industry would have to invent [it] or be dead."[39]

More recently, TIRC and its successor organization, the Council for Tobacco Research, have been attacked as the headquarters of an industry cartel to keep firms in line.

EXECUTIVE: If it was a cartel, it just didn't work.

MODERATOR: Why do you say that?

EXECUTIVE: Just look at how furiously we competed throughout the 1950s to develop and market filter cigarettes in response to the trumped-up "cancer scare": Lorillard introduced its filtered Kent; R.J. Reynolds introduced its filtered Winston; Philip Morris introduced its filtered Marlboro; sales of Brown & Williamson's filtered Viceroy skyrocketed.[40] In 1953, filtered cigarettes accounted for less than 3 percent of all cigarette sales. But by 1958—owing to fierce competition to offer consumers what they wanted—filters accounted for nearly half the entire market, eventually reaching 94 percent by the 1980s.[41] That's a pretty lousy way to run a cartel!

MODERATOR: I gather these health skirmishes proceeded throughout the 1950s, but that the truly defining moment came in 1964.

HISTORIAN: Yes, 1964 was a watershed. That's when the landmark report early that year by the Surgeon General's Advisory Committee on Smoking and Health was published. Its conclusion—arrived at by consensus among a prestigious panel that assessed all available evidence in a deliberately conservative way—immediately attracted national attention: "Cigarette smoking," the report declared, "is a health hazard of sufficient importance in the United States to warrant appropriate remedial action."[42] It blew the health side of the tobacco wars sky-high.

EXECUTIVE: Overlooked, however, was the fact that the surgeon general's report was based on the smoking of *un*filtered cigarettes, which, as I just indicated, were rapidly disappearing in favor of the filtered cigarettes we were rushing to introduce.

It also is an axiom of elementary statistical analysis that correlation doesn't prove causation. Just because tobacco consumption and cancer might parallel each other does not imply that one necessarily causes the other. After all, over the same time period car ownership, the number of ballpoint pens sold, and the number of telephones per capita also increased. These, too, would be highly correlated with the incidence of cancer over that time frame, but no one would contend that any of these *caused* cancer.[43] The surgeon general's 1964 report was emphatic on this point: It stated categorically: "Statistical methods cannot establish proof of a causal relationship in an association. The causal significance of an association is a matter of judgment which goes beyond any statement of statistical probability."[44]

Our industry discharged its duty of educating the public to this key fact and informed them that a variety of variables, in addition to tobacco consumption, affect the incidence of cancer.

HISTORIAN: Nevertheless, a clear turning point had been reached: As Graphic 1-2 shows, the U.S. smoking rate steadily declined after 1963, dropping from 40 percent of adults in 1965 to 25 percent more recently.

Simultaneously, the tobacco wars dramatically escalated:

A flood of surgeon general reports were subsequently issued, calling attention to an expanding number of smoking health hazards, including threats to fetal development during pregnancy and the dangers of secondhand smoke inhaled by nonsmokers. These reports culminated in 1984 when C. Everett Koop, President Reagan's surgeon general, called for a "Smoke-Free Society" by the year 2000.[45]

Beginning in 1965, a succession of federal laws mandated ever stronger health warnings on tobacco packages and advertisements.[46]

The Public Health Smoking Act enacted in 1970 banned cigarette advertising in the broadcast media beginning in 1971.[47]

Nonsmoking sections on commercial airline flights and other forms of public transportation were mandated by government decree beginning in 1971.

And many states and communities have enacted regulations that have expanded smoking restrictions almost everywhere—restaurants, workplaces, offices, hotels, elevators, cultural and sports facilities, hospitals, and so forth.[48]

MODERATOR: Yet, aren't we in the midst of a cigar craze?

HISTORIAN: You're absolutely right. U.S. cigar consumption has jumped 45 percent just since 1993.

EXECUTIVE: It underscores how unpredictable smoking habits really are.

MODERATOR: Smoking among young people has become extremely controversial.

HISTORIAN: That, too, has come to play a very important role in the growing war on tobacco. The Centers for Disease Control estimate that over one-third of all high school students were smokers in 1995, up from one-quarter in 1991. Each day, more than 3,000 young people experiment with tobacco consumption, adding more than a million new young smokers annually. In fact, it is estimated that more than three-quarters of all smokers begin smoking before they are 18.[49] With confidential company documents revealing that tobacco firms intricately examine the behavior and smoking proclivities of youngsters—including children as young as 5—and that they tailor their marketing and advertising to target them in order to replenish their shrinking customer base,[50] the youth issue has certainly added fuel to the antismoking fire.

MODERATOR: Can you provide a specific example?

HISTORIAN: Certainly. Look at the intense jockeying between Philip Morris and R. J. Reynolds to dominate the youth segment of the market: Reynolds created its Joe Camel campaign in the late-1980s in an attempt to dent Marlboro's 75 percent share of the 18-to-24-year-old youth market. Camel's sales to that age segment subsequently climbed 64 percent, and the two firms have hotly competed for that particular field.[51]

EXECUTIVE: I and my executive colleagues were completely unaware. We are shocked and ashamed by the revelations that are now coming to light. They represent rare lapses in judgment on the part of our subordinates. We categorically do not believe children should be the targets of our marketing efforts, and we have so stated publicly.[52]

MODERATOR: All of this culminating in the spectacular settlement proposed in June 1997 between 40 states and the industry?

HISTORIAN: Yes. Some states have prosecuted their own individual lawsuits against the industry to recover what they contend are government medical expenses caused by smoking. And some of these suits have been settled for very large amounts: Mississippi, $3.4 billion; Florida, $11.3 billion; Texas, $15.3 billion; Minnesota, $6.6 billion.

EXECUTIVE: A bonanza for lawyers working on a contingency fee basis and reaping billion-dollar paydays!

HISTORIAN: Transcending these individual legal actions, as you indicate, is the epic multistate settlement proposed in 1997. ~~Had it been adopted, it would have empowered the Food and Drug Administration to regulate tobacco as a "Class A Carcinogen";~~ drastically curtailed advertising and marketing of tobacco; imposed strict licensing requirements and regulations on retailers of tobacco products; and dramatically expanded restrictions on smoking in order to virtually eliminate exposure to cigarette smoke by nonsmokers.

If adopted, it also would have established strict timelines for reducing smoking among young people by 60 percent over a 10-year period and imposed financial penalties on producers if these reductions weren't achieved.

Not least, the industry would have been obligated to pay $368.5 billion in fines over a 25-year period to fund the foregoing programs along with a variety of other antismoking initiatives.

Since coming before the Congress in early 1998, that original settlement became a football in a fierce political fight to amend it: whether to drop immunity from prosecution for tobacco companies; whether to vastly increase the financial penalties imposed; and whether to decree sharper reductions in youth smoking rates.

EXECUTIVE: The only public benefit of that settlement would have been to provide my industry a respite from frivolous class action lawsuits filed by fast-buck lawyers and publicity hungry public officials!

HISTORIAN: As initially proposed, it would have also permitted you to deduct all expenses and fines from your corporate taxes, putting the ultimate financial burden in the laps of American taxpayers.

EXECUTIVE: If I could return to the overall trends of recent decades, I contend that they mark an astonishing national hysteria—a 30-year assault on the basic liberties of the American people—during which antismoking zealotry has masqueraded as moderation in the destruction of personal freedom. It's come to a point where crack addicts get more sympathy than smokers unable to resist a cigarette.[53]

MODERATOR: Many would consider that quite an exaggeration.

EXECUTIVE: But it's not. Take the case of airline flights: As our economic historian points out, the first federal law on this subject required smokers to sit in designated smoking areas.

MODERATOR: Given the eye-watering consequences of sitting next to a smoker, that seems reasonable.

EXECUTIVE: Viewed alone and in isolation, I would agree with you. But that wasn't the end of it.

Following their initial success, antismoking radicals next lobbied government to ban smoking entirely on all domestic flights—but "only," they said, on flights of less than two hours' duration. Were they satisfied? No! They next demanded that government extend the ban to *all* domestic flights, *regardless* of duration. This, they said, was "reasonable" because it would apply "only" to domestic flights. Now that they've gotten that, will they be satisfied? Of course not—they'll be demanding that governments ban smoking on all *international* flights, too. And they'll present their case as "reasonable" because interplanetary space flight will remain unaffected!

When I consider this from my own long-run perspective, I don't think it's paranoid to suspect that today's bans on smoking in private offices are a short step away from laws forbidding people from smoking in their own homes—and a step away from the police state needed to enforce that kind of all-encompassing ban.

MODERATOR: From nonsmoking airline flights to a police state? Aren't you now really stretching things?

EXECUTIVE: I don't think so. Do you realize that some antismoking groups are now suggesting that parents who smoke at home be prosecuted for engaging in "child abuse," and that their children be forcibly taken from them by the state?[54] In their deluded quest for eternal life, are antismoking baby boomers going to transform the country into one big gulag? Put one quarter of our adult population in prison? Force children of smokers into mass orphanages?

Some employers are beginning to subject employees to urine tests in order to determine if they smoke.[55]

I ask, very seriously, where does this end?

HISTORIAN: You may find these anecdotal tidbits amusing. The fact remains that cigarettes kill. The tobacco companies manufacture and sell a lethal product that nets them handsome profits. In the final analysis, however, the taxpayer is forced to foot the bill for dealing with its deleterious consequences.

MODERATOR: I'm afraid our viewers will have to answer some of these questions for themselves, because we've run out of time.

I want to thank our guests for providing a lively survey of the issues that our series will explore in depth over the next four weeks.

In closing, perhaps we can all agree with George Bernard Shaw's observation that "it is difficult for smokers and nonsmokers to share the same railway car."

Please join us next week, when we analyze the skirmishes on the consumer front in the tobacco wars.

REFERENCES

[1] U.S. Food and Drug Administration (FDA), "Children and Tobacco: The Facts," press release, Aug. 10, 1995.

[2] Kenneth E. Warner, "Till Death Do Us Part: America's Turbulent Love Affair with the Cigarette," *1990 Medical and Health Annual,* ed. E. Bernstein (Chicago: Encyclopedia Britannica, 1989), p. 75.

[3] U.S. Congress, Office of Technology Assessment, *Smoking-Related Deaths and Financial Costs,* 1993.

[4] State of Florida v. American Tobacco Co., No. CL95-1466AH, Dec. 13, 1996).

[5] U.S. Department of Health and Human Services, *Smoking and Health in the Americas: A 1992 Report of the Surgeon General in Collaboration with the Pan American Health Organization,* (Washington, GPO, 1992) pp. 20–21.

[6] Quoted in Sherwin J. Feinhandler, "The Social Role of Smoking," in *Smoking and Society,* ed. Robert Tollison (Lexington, MA: Lexington Books, 1986), p. 170.

[7] Richard D. Kluger, *Ashes to Ashes* (New York: Vintage Books, 1997), p. 9.

[8] Ilene Barth, *The Smoking Life* (Columbus, MS: Genesis Press, 1997), p. 8.

[9] Nicolo Menardes, *Joyfull Newes of our Newe Founde Worlde,* trans. J. Frampton (New York: Knopf, 1925).

[10] Feinhandler, "Social Role of Smoking," p. 175.

[11] Barth, *Smoking Life,* p. 19; W. Kip Viscusi, *Smoking: Making the Risky Decision* (New York: Oxford University Press, 1992), p. 47.

[12] Kluger, *Ashes to Ashes,* p. 15.

[13] Barth, *Smoking Life,* p. 21.

[14] Jacob Sullum, *For Your Own Good: The Anti-Smoking Crusade and the Tyranny of Public Health* (New York: Free Press, 1998), pp. 18–23.

[15] Barth, *Smoking Life,* pp. 163–164; Kluger, *Ashes to Ashes,* p. 12.

[16] U.S. Bureau of the Census, *Statistical Abstract of the United States: 1997,* pp. 752, 809; Centers for Disease Control, *1995 Household Survey on Drug Abuse* (August 1996).

[17] U.S. Department of Health and Human Services, *Smoking and Health in the Americas,* p. 30.

[18] W. Kip Viscusi, "From Cash Crop to Cash Cow: How Tobacco Profits State Governments," *Regulation* (summer 1997), p. 28; U.S. Bureau of the Census, *Statistical Abstract of the United States: 1997,* pp. 309, 333.

[19] "CCH Update on Cigarette Taxes," *Action on Smoking and Health (ASH),* February 2, 1998.

[20] Christopher Georges & Jackie Calmes, "Clinton to Seek Boost in Prices of Tobacco," *The Wall Street Journal*, Jan. 8, 1998, p. A3.

[21] Feinhandler, "Social Role of Smoking," p. 171.

[22] Kluger, *Ashes to Ashes*, p. 13.

[23] Feinhandler, "Social Role of Smoking," p. 174.

[24] United States v. American Tobacco Co., 221 U.S. 106, 156–57 (1911); Henry R. Seager and Charles A. Gulick, *Trust and Corporation Problems* (New York: Harper & Bros., 1929), p. 150.

[25] Richard B. Tenant, *The American Cigarette Industry* (New Haven, CT: Yale University Press, 1950), p. 27.

[26] United States v. American Tobacco Co., 221 U.S. 106 (1911).

[27] American Tobacco Co. v. United States, 328 U.S. 781 (1946).

[28] "More Counties to Sue Cigarette Makers," *Action on Smoking and Health (ASH)*, February 27, 1998.

[29] Barth, *Smoking Life*, p. 24; Viscusi, "Cash Crop," p. 47; U.S. Department of Health and Human Services, *Smoking and Health in the Americas*, p. 30.

[30] R. A. Radford, "The Economic Organization of a P.O.W. Camp," 12 *Economica* (1945): 189–201.

[31] Barth, *Smoking Life*, p. 42.

[32] Sullum, *Your Own Good*, pp. 31, 33.

[33] U.S. Department of Health and Human Services, Centers for Disease Control, Office on Smoking and Health, *Reducing the Health Consequences of Smoking: 25 Years of Progress*, (Washington, DC: GPO, 1989), p. 268.

[34] E.L. Wynder, E.A. Graham and A.B. Croninger, "Experimental Production of Carcinoma with Cigarette Tar," *Cancer Research*, (1953): 855–64.

[35] See R. Doll and A.B. Hill, "A Study of the Aetiology of Carcinoma of the Lung," 2 *British Medical Journal* (1952): 1271–86; idem, "The Mortality of Doctors in Relation to Their Smoking Habits: A Preliminary Report," 1 *British Medical Journal*, (1954): 1451–55; E.C. Hammond and D. Horn, "The Relationship Between Human Smoking Habits and Death Rates," 155 *Journal of the American Medical Association* (1954): 1316–28.

The surgeon general's 1964 *Report*, Chapters 9–12, contains an exhaustive survey of these and other medical studies. These findings were prominently publicized by *The Reader's Digest* in the early 1950s. See C. W. Lieb, "Can the Poisons in Cigarettes Be Avoided?" *The Reader's Digest*, December 1953, pp. 45–47; L. M. Miller and J. Monahan, "The Facts Behind the Cigarette Controversy," *The Reader's Digest*, July 1954, pp. 1–6; and R. Norr, "Cancer by the Carton," *The Reader's Digest*, Dec. 1952, pp. 7–8.

[36] Kluger, *Ashes to Ashes*, p. 162.

[37] Quoted in Alix M. Freedman and Laurie P. Cohen, "How Cigarette Makers Keep Health Question 'Open' Year After Year," *The Wall Street Journal*, Feb. 11, 1993, p. 1.

[38] Ibid.

[39] State of Minnesota v. Philip Morris Inc., Trial Exhibit No. 10,197.

[40] Richard B. Tenant, "The Cigarette Industry," in *The Structure of American Industry*, 4th ed., Walter Adams ed., (New York: Macmillan, 1971), p. 229.

[41] U.S. Department of Health and Human Services, Public Health Service, Office on Smoking and Health, *The Health Consequences of Smoking for Women: A Report of the Surgeon General*, (Washington, DC: GPO, 1986), p. 21; idem, *25 Years of Progress*, p. 314.

[42] U.S. Department of Health, Education, and Welfare, *Smoking and Health: Report of the Advisory Committee to the Surgeon General of the Public Health Service* (Washington, DC: GPO, 1964), p. 33.

[43] Hans J. Eysenck, "Smoking and Health," in *Smoking and Society,* Robert D. Tollison ed., (Lexington, MA: Lexington Books, 1986), p. 23.

[44] Department of Health, Education, and Welfare, *Smoking and Health*, p. 20.

[45] Capsule summaries of many of these reports are presented in U.S. Department of Health and Human Services, *Reducing the Health Consequences of Smoking*, pp. 8–10.

[46] Ibid., pp. 477–78.

[47] Ibid., p. 511.

[48] For one detailed survey of state and local antismoking policies, see U.S. Department of Health and Human Services, Centers for Disease Control, *Smoking and Health: A National Status Report*, (Washington, DC: GPO, 1990).

[49] U.S. Congress. Senate. Committee on Commerce, Science, and Transportation. *Hearing on Tobacco Advertising, Marketing, and Labeling*, 105th Cong., 2d sess., March 3, 1998 (testimony of Michael P. Eriksen, Office on Smoking and Health, Centers for Disease Control and Prevention).

[50] See Milo Geyelin, "Release of Tobacco Documents Ordered," *The Wall Street Journal*, March 9, 1998, p. A3, and Barry Meier, "Files of R. J. Reynolds Tobacco Show Efforts on Youths," *New York Times*, January 15, 1998, p. A10.

[51] Karren Mills, "Joe Camel Unable to Get Out from Under Marlboro Man," Associated Press, Apr. 4, 1998.

[52] Bill Dedman, "Tobacco Executive 'Ashamed' of Attention to Young Smokers," *New York Times*, March 4, 1998, p. A12.

[53] See Mike Barnicle, "The Price of a Cigarette," *Boston Globe,* Mar. 2, 1998, p. B1.

[54] "Smokers Risking Children's Lives," *Action on Smoking and Health (ASH),* Nov. 8, 1997; "No Right to Smoke Around Child," Nov. 6, 1997 (Web site).

[55] U.S. Congress. House. Subcommittee on Health and the Environment. *Environmental Tobacco Smoke: Hearing Before the House Subcommittee on Health and the Environment,* 103d Cong., 1st sess., 1993, pp. 5–6 (statement of Rep. Thomas J. Bliley, "EPA and Environmental Smoke: Science of Politics.")

II. The Consumer Front

MODERATOR: Welcome to the second program in our five-part series, *The Tobacco Wars.*

    Tonight we focus on the consumer's role in making cigarettes one of the largest consumer goods industries in the United States—and one of the most lucrative.

    Consumers spend some $50 billion each year on tobacco products. Why? Aren't they aware of the health risks of smoking? Are they behaving rationally in assessing the costs and benefits of indulging their cravings for tobacco? Does addiction cloud their judgment? Can significant price hikes cut their tobacco consumption?

    To explore these questions we are joined tonight by three panelists: a representative from each of the country's leading pro- and antitobacco advocacy groups, and an economist who specializes in the theory of consumer behavior.

    Welcome to all of you, and thank you for joining us. At the outset, let's put these issues in perspective by examining the relevant statistics. First, how widespread is tobacco consumption in America?

PROTOBACCO: I'd be delighted to respond to that question because I think our viewers will be surprised by the numbers: some 50 million adults are smokers in the United States.[1] To put it in perspective, consider that it's approximately equal to the population of the entire northeastern United States—including New

York, New Jersey, and Pennsylvania!—and only a few million shy of the population of the entire western United States or the midwestern states.

MODERATOR: What fraction of the population does that represent?

PROTOBACCO: It represents approximately one quarter of the country's adult population.[2]

MODERATOR: Does the smoking rate vary across geographical regions?

PROTOBACCO: Somewhat. It ranges from 32 percent in the north central section of the country to 26 percent in the West. By urban area, the rate varies from 27 percent in large metropolitan areas to 33 percent in rural areas[3]—again, a very sizable segment of the population.

MODERATOR: How does tobacco consumption compare for various racial and ethnic groups?

PROTOBACCO: Smoking rates are quite similar for African-American adults and white adults, at a rate of approximately 26 percent. The rate for Hispanic adults, however, is a notch lower, on the order of 19 percent.[4]

MODERATOR: Are there any significant differences in the smoking behavior of men and women?

PROTOBACCO: In earlier decades, yes, there were substantial differences; far fewer women smoked than men, and those who did began smoking much later in life. Widespread smoking among women lagged behind the peak year for men by about a quarter of a century. ~~Since the 1970s, however, their smoking rates have converged.~~[5]

ANTITOBACCO: So has their incidence of lung cancer.[6] For each of the past 11 years, lung cancer has exceeded breast cancer as a cause of death among women[7]—just one of a mountain of significant facts neglected by prosmoking groups.

MODERATOR: Such as?

ANTITOBACCO: ~~Such as that 10 million people in the United States have died from smoking-related causes since the surgeon general's 1964 report.~~ Two million of those deaths—a number exceeding the entire population of Houston—are attributed to lung cancer alone.[8]
~~Projecting these death rates into the future, former Surgeon General Koop describes them as the annual equivalent of "1,000 jumbo jets emblazoned with Marlboro and Winston and Camel insignia crashing each year for the next three decades."~~[9]

PROTOBACCO: Six times as many people died from all causes over the same period. The inescapable reality is that the mortality rate for all people, ultimately, is one hundred percent.

ANTITOBACCO: It's a waste of life when 1.5 million Americans become newly addicted to smoking every year. Let's look at the statistics for young Americans: Twenty percent of young people between the ages of 12 and 17 are smokers—~~one-fifth of the nation's~~ ~~children hooked on tobacco!~~[10] Eighty-two percent of adult smokers had their first cigarette before the age of 18.[11] Some 3,000 children try smoking every day, with 1,000 of these eventually becoming addicts. Between 1991 and 1994, the smoking rate among eighth-graders in this country increased 30 percent.[12] These are alarming facts.

MODERATOR: Can we put these American statistics in some kind of global perspective? How does the U.S. smoking rate compare with the rest of the world?

PROTOBACCO: An excellent question. Despite antismoker efforts to portray America as a country suffocated by cigarette smoke, the fact is that smoking is far more widespread in the rest of the world: In South Korea, for example, approximately 70 percent of all men smoke, while in China and Japan, the figure is approximately 60 percent. In the formerly communist countries of Central and Eastern Europe, the smoking rate is also around 60 percent.

Overall, of 87 nations for which data are available, the United States ranks 78th in the rate at which its people smoke. Put differently, only 9 of nearly 90 nations worldwide have lower smoking rates than the United States.[13]

ANTITOBACCO: There is another side to these global statistics: Over recent decades, smoking rates for developed countries have dropped sizably and steadily. In the United States, the rate has plunged from more than 50 percent during the 1950s to a 25 percent range in recent years.

It is only in the less developed nations where the smoking rate has risen.[14] So I suppose if underdevelopment is your ideal, then you can take comfort in these global statistics. But that's not how the World Health Organization sees it. The subtitle of their study was *A Global Health Emergency.* And no wonder. To quote from the study, "Every ten seconds, another person dies as a result of tobacco use. Tobacco products are estimated to have caused around 3 million deaths a year in the early 1990s, and the death toll is steadily increasing. Unless current smoking trends are reversed," the study warns, "that figure is expected to rise to 10 million deaths per year by the 2020s or early 2030s, with 70 percent of those deaths occurring in developing countries."[15]

PROTOBACCO: Correlation is not causation! I doubt anyone would argue that a reduction in the smoking rate alone would transform an impoverished nation into an economic Shangri-la. Ensuring sanitary water supplies and combating death from malaria should take precedence over propagating first-world antismoking fads.[16]

MODERATOR: Since we've broached the health issue, let's address it squarely: Why do antismoking groups consider tobacco consumption hazardous to our health? What are the death and disease risks?

ANTITOBACCO: As the old saying has it, a picture is worth a thousand words. The mortality statistics depicted in Graphic 2-1 tell the story.

MODERATOR: Please interpret these statistics for us.

ANTITOBACCO: These are relative risk ratios, indicating the statistical rate at which each disease afflicts smokers, divided by the corresponding rate at which each afflicts people who don't smoke.

MODERATOR: So a relative risk ratio of 2 would indicate that smokers were twice as likely as nonsmokers to contract a particular disease?

ANTITOBACCO: That's right. These statistics are both dreadful and astonishing. They reveal, for example, that male smokers are 22 times more likely to contract lung cancer than nonsmokers; 9.6 times more likely to suffer from emphysema and other pulmonary diseases than nonsmokers; and 7-10 times more likely to suffer cancer of the throat and larynx.
      Female smokers also incur highly elevated risks. They are 10.4 times more likely to contract emphysema than nonsmoking women; 17.7 times more likely to suffer cancer of the larynx; and 11.9 times more likely to acquire lung cancer.

MODERATOR: I believe you have some additional statistics to show us?

GRAPHIC 2-1

RELATIVE RISKS OF SMOKING-ASSOCIATED DISEASES

	Male		Female	
Cause of Death	**Current Smoker**	**Former Smoker**	**Current Smoker**	**Former Smoker**
All causes	2.34	1.58	1.90	1.32
Coronary heart disease*	1.94	1.41	1.78	1.31
Other heart disease	1.85	1.32	1.69	1.16
Cerebrovascular lesions*	2.24	1.29	1.84	1.06
Other circulatory disease	4.06	2.33	3.00	1.34
Chronic obstructive pulmonary disease	9.65	8.75	10.47	7.04
Other respiratory disease	1.99	1.56	2.18	1.38
Cancer (lip, oral cavity, pharynx)	27.48	8.80	5.59	2.88
Cancer (esophagus)	7.60	5.83	10.25	3.16
Cancer (larynx)	10.48	5.24	17.78	11.88
Cancer (lung)	22.36	9.36	11.94	4.69
Cancer (bladder, urinary organs)	2.86	1.90	2.58	1.85

*Ages 35 years and up.

Source: U.S. Department of Health and Human Services, "Reducing the Health Consequences of Smoking: 25 Years of Progress" *Report of the Surgeon General, Office on Smoking and Health,* (Washington, DC: GPO, 1989), pp. 150–51.

ANTITOBACCO: Yes. Graphic 2-2 illustrates the health hazards of smoking in a different way. It reveals, for example, that 45 percent of coronary heart disease among all men aged 35 through 64 is attributable to smoking. And just look at the statistics for lung cancer: 90 percent of lung cancer among all men is caused by smoking with a 79 percent rate of smoking-induced lung cancer among women.

These statistics irrefutably demonstrate that smoking kills.

MODERATOR: Since you put it that way, can you give us some idea of how smoking compares with some other causes of death?

ANTITOBACCO: Yes, that is indicated in Graphic 2-3, depicting the risk of death from various causes. Obviously, smoking is by far the most lethal activity in which people engage.

PROTOBACCO: Deception with statistics is a venerable craft, which antismoking groups have perfected into a fine art form.

MODERATOR: In what way?

PROTOBACCO: In almost every way. First, as I indicated earlier, it is an axiom of statistics that correlation does not establish causality. The number of personal computers and illegitimate births have increased together, but no one would contend that one has "caused" the other. The correlation between them is entirely spurious.

GRAPHIC 2-2

SMOKING-ATTRIBUTABLE FRACTION FOR
TEN SELECTED CAUSES OF DEATH,
UNITED STATES, 1985

Cause of death	Men (%)	Women (%)
Coronary heart disease (aged 35-64)	45	41
Coronary heart disease aged ≥ 65)	21	12
Cerebrovascular disease (aged 35-64)	51	55
Cerebrovascular disease (aged ≥ 65)	24	6
Cancer of the lung	90	79
Cancer of the lip, oral cavity, and pharynx	92	61
Cancer of the larynx	81	87
Cancer of the esophagus	78	75
Cancer of the pancreas	29	34
Cancer of the bladder	47	37
Cancer of the kidney	48	12
Chronic obstructive pulmonary disease	84	79

Source: U.S. Department of Health and Human Services, Public Health Service, Office on Smoking and Health, *Smoking and Health in the Americas,* (Washington, DC: GPO, 1992), p. 89.

GRAPHIC 2-3

ESTIMATED RISKS OF VARIOUS ACTIVITIES

Activity or cause	Annual fatalities per 1 million exposed persons
Active smoking	7,000[a]
Alcohol	541
Accident	275
Disease	266
Motor vehicles	187
Alcohol-involved	95
Non-alcohol-involved	92
Work	113
Swimming	22
Passive smoking[b]	19
All other air pollutants[b]	6
Football	6
Electrocution	2
Lightning	0.5
DES in cattlefeed	0.3
Bee sting	0.2
Basketball	0.02

[a] Number of deaths per million smokers who began smoking before 1965.
[b] Cancer deaths only.

Source: U.S. Department of Health and Human Services, Public Health Service, Office on Smoking and Health, *Reducing the Health Consequences of Smoking: 25 Years of Progress* (Washington, DC: GPO, 1989), p. 160.

Likewise, disease and death trends are subject to influence by a large array of factors, including atmospheric pollution, demographic variables, increased use of pharmaceutical drugs, methods of food production and consumption, genetic damage by mutagens, and so forth.[17] Smoking is only one of a large, complex, and unknown number of factors at work.

Second, there are numerous diseases whose incidence is *less* for smokers than for nonsmokers—that is, the relative risk ratio is *less* than 1. These include colorectal cancers, primary central nervous system neoplasms, Parkinson's disease, and diabetes.[18] In these cases, according to the antismokers' methodology, *not* smoking is dangerous to your health!

MODERATOR: Do you have other criticisms of the smoking-health statistics?

PROTOBACCO Yes. They are fundamentally misleading and distorted, and they exaggerate the health risks immensely. Note that all the statistics in Graphic 2-1 are expressed in terms of *relative* risk. They purport to tell us that smokers are ten times more likely to die from this, and six times more likely to die from that. But what they hide is the absolute risk of disease or death attributable to smoking.

MODERATOR: How would the absolute risk statistics change the picture?

PROTOBACCO: In the following way: the Centers for Disease Control claim that something on the order of

420,000 deaths each year are supposedly "due" to smoking.[19] That represents less than 1 percent of the 50 million people who smoke. So, expressed in terms of this absolute risk, a smoker's chances of living are 99 in 100. Those are rather favorable odds!

Similarly, statistics on lung cancer can be presented in a different way in order to expose the degree to which antismokers exaggerate the alleged relationship. To listen to antismokers, you might suppose that lung cancer accounts for a huge proportion of deaths each year. But the fact is that it doesn't. Lung cancer represents less than 7 percent of the total deaths due to all causes in the United States every year.[20]

It's just not the catastrophic epidemic that the antismokers would have us believe.

MODERATOR: What does your organization estimate a more accurate figure to be for death and disease attributable to smoking?

PROTOBACCO: We calculate it to be on the order of one-half or less of the artificially inflated figure promulgated by antismoking organizations.[21]

Express the data that way and all the antismoking hue and cry is seen for what it really is—one of the greatest hoaxes ever perpetrated on the American public.

ANTITOBACCO: What you fail to mention is that tobacco is a "gateway" drug, and that smokers are 4 times more likely to abuse alcohol and engage in illicit drug use—8 to 11 times more likely in the case of teens.

Nor do you indicate that smoking is *negatively* correlated with education: a 17 percent smoking rate for college-educated people versus 37 percent for non-college-educated.[22] That statistic is very telling, I think. It holds across racial and ethnic lines.

PROTOBACCO: Surely you're not suggesting that smokers are mentally handicapped?

ANTITOBACCO: I'm suggesting the statistics show that the more educated people are far less likely to smoke.

PROTOBACCO: Some of my smoking friends have Ph.D.'s.

ANTITOBACCO: I trust our viewers won't confuse academic credentials with intelligence. I subscribe to Horace Greeley's definition of a cigar as a fire at one end and a fool at the other.

MODERATOR: All right folks, with these various statistics as background let's move on to the next major question. *Why* do people consume tobacco products? Why do they smoke? What is their motivation?

PROTOBACCO: That's a fascinating question—one that has occupied researchers for many decades, and to which there is no generally accepted answer.

Some researchers attribute tobacco consumption to sociological factors. For example, because a smoker is readily accepted into a circle of other smokers, smoking may serve as a means for breaking down social barriers. By the same token, smoking may be a way of reinforcing and reaffirming relationships among existing members of a particular group. Offering a cigarette or accepting a light may also promote "bonding" and cement social relationships.[23]

Other researchers explain smoking behavior on psychological grounds. Smoking may be a way of combating boredom. It may mitigate emotional stress and anxiety. People may smoke when they feel good or, alternatively, when they're down in the dumps and need a lift. Interestingly, some people may smoke because it relaxes them, while others may smoke because it stimulates them and perks them up. Some clear personality differences also have been found to distinguish smokers from nonsmokers; for example, smokers tend as a group to be more extroverted, more gregarious, more active and energetic, and even more productive.[24]

Still other explanations revolve around sensory pleasure—people smoke because they enjoy the taste, the feel, the experience.

ANTITOBACCO: Let's cut through all the psychobabble! People consume tobacco because they're addicted to the nicotine it contains. The tobacco companies have known this for years, as their heretofore secret documents amply attest.

For example, here's how a Philip Morris researcher confidentially explained the behavior of smokers: "The product is nicotine"; the cigarette pack is "a storage container for a day's supply of nicotine"; the cigarette is "a dispenser for a dose unit of nicotine"; and the puff of smoke is "the vehicle of nicotine." "As with eating and copulating," he explained, "so it is with smoking. The physiological effect"—that is, nicotine addiction—"serves as the primary incentive; all other incentives are secondary."[25]

And this wasn't the view of just one person at one tobacco company. Here's how it was explained at R. J. Reynolds: "Nicotine is known to be a habit-forming alkaloid, hence the confirmed user of tobacco products is primarily seeking the physiological 'satisfaction' derived from nicotine. . . . Thus a tobacco product is, in essence, a vehicle for delivery of nicotine. . . . Our industry is then based upon design, manufacture and sale of attractive dosage forms of nicotine."[26]

Tobacco consumption is a fatal addiction, which all the pseudoscientific, psychoso-ciological rationalizations in the world can't mask.

PROTOBACCO: Your cultural insensitivity shocks me! To quote from a recent surgeon general's report, "Since prehistoric times, tobacco has been part of the life and culture of the Americas and has been a prominent feature of the religious and healing practices of the region's indigenous societies."[27] For the Tupinamba Indians of Brazil, smoke blown in each others' faces was a ritual for instilling courage to overcome one's enemies—a practice not without appeal under current circumstances.[28]

In fact, tobacco continues to be smoked around the world in a variety of social and cultural contexts: Pacific Island courtship rituals; African councils and clan gatherings; North and South American Indian healing ceremonies; at the conclusion of contractual negotiations in various regions of Asia; and as a form of hospitality in some parts of the Middle East.[29]

MODERATOR: Professor, perhaps you can help us. You specialize in the economic theory of consumer behavior. You've been listening to our discussion. So let me ask you: How can economic theory explain why people consume tobacco products?

ECONOMIST: Utility.

MODERATOR: A single-word response doesn't seem to get us very far.

ECONOMIST: On the contrary, the economic theory underlying that word explains everything that people do or buy or consume—including smoking.

MODERATOR: Please elaborate for us.

ECONOMIST: Economic theory posits that people behave rationally. And what "rational" behavior means is that people have an ultimate end or objective in mind, and that they consciously assess every action they might take in terms of its contribution to their sense of utility.

MODERATOR: Just what is this all-purpose thing called "utility"?

ECONOMIST: Perhaps Jeremy Bentham, the father of utilitarianism, put it best some two hundred years ago. "By utility," he wrote, "is meant that property in any object, whereby it tends to produce benefit, advantage, pleasure, good, or happiness."[30] Put differently, it's a person's sense of his or her own well-being or satisfaction.

MODERATOR: That seems rather abstract.

ECONOMIST: Let's make it more concrete. Consider an apple: its utility for one person might be its color. For another person, its utility might stem from the taste. A third person might derive utility from the adage that consuming an apple a day keeps the doctor away. And once upon a time—certainly long before my time—a student might obtain a sense of well-being, or utility, from the hope that an apple left on the professor's desk would result in a better grade.

MODERATOR: But if "utility" means so many different things to different people, how can it serve as the basis for explaining the behavior of any single individual? Can you economists measure or weigh it?

ECONOMIST: No. We can't even compare it across individuals. But we don't need to be able to do any of those things. The theory holds that individuals are rational beings who know what utility means for them individually. Each person has his or her own likes and dislikes—"tastes and preferences" in economic vernacular.

Given the amount of their income, and given the prices they must pay for each product, the theory tells us that individuals will purchase the goods that provide them the greatest additional utility relative to the price they must pay. Behaving rationally, they'll consume the bundle of goods and services that provide them the greatest utility "bang per buck."

As Bentham put it, there has never been a human creature, "however stupid or perverse," who does not behave according to this principle, usually without even thinking about it.[31]

So to return to your question, people smoke because, according to economic theory, it maximizes their utility.

MODERATOR: How can we be certain of that?

ECONOMIST: If smoking doesn't maximize their utility, and they're rational, then they will choose not to smoke.

MODERATOR: So in economic parlance, those who smoke do so because it makes them better off, while others don't smoke because it provides them little or no utility?

ECONOMIST: Precisely. Their behavior reveals their preferences.

PROTOBACCO: The professor makes a profoundly important point that antismoking groups refuse to admit —namely, the choice to smoke is a rational decision made by millions of intelligent people.

ANTITOBACCO: I don't see how that statement can possibly be justified. The statistics I cited earlier show that the American smoking rate has *dropped* immensely over the past 40 years. If anything, that trend demonstrates what tobacco's defenders refuse to admit: when people are adequately informed about the dangers of smoking, they rationally choose *not* to do it!

MODERATOR: What about it, Professor? Which group is right here? Which side represents rationality and sweet reason?

ECONOMIST: Well, from a theoretical perspective, *both* sides can be correct.

MODERATOR: How can that possibly be?

ECONOMIST: The economic theory is quite general. What you must understand is that every person has his or her own tastes and preferences—his or her own likes and dislikes. No two people are exactly the same in this critical respect. As a result, this innate sense of utility will vary among different individuals.

They may all confront the same prices for various goods and services. And they may even have the same incomes. But differences in their tastes and preferences can lead them to make different consumption choices.

It's not a question of smokers being right and nonsmokers being wrong, or vice versa. Rather, both groups can be behaving rationally given their different tastes and preferences.

MODERATOR: How does your economic theory explain the decline in smoking that we've seen in recent decades?

ECONOMIST: In a fairly straightforward fashion. As information has been disseminated about the health risks of smoking, those adverse consequences have been rationally interpreted by many people as effectively raising the "price" of smoking. That is, the price now not only includes the monetary outlay per pack but also the possibility of contracting a host of smoking-related diseases. Knowledge of these adverse health effects, in effect, raises the price to the consumer of smoking. And this price increase, in turn, results in a decline in the quantity of cigarettes consumed— precisely what we've observed.

MODERATOR: Is there any evidence to corroborate that theory?

ECONOMIST: Quite a lot, actually. Smoking rates dipped noticeably in the early 1950s following the first national attention to medical studies finding a link between smoking and lung cancer. Similar declines in smoking rates occurred following publication of the surgeon general's 1964 smoking report as well as in the late 1960s with the advent of government-mandated warning labels and "Fairness Doctrine" rulings by the Federal Communications Commission requiring broadcasters to air antismoking messages in response to cigarette ads.[32]

MODERATOR: But if that's the case, how does your economic theory account for the fact that 50 million Americans continue to smoke, despite three decades of adverse medical findings and health warnings?

ECONOMIST: Again, it all goes back to the concept that each person makes his or her own choice. Smokers consider the benefits of smoking—the utility—to outweigh the price of smoking, including the health dangers, so they smoke. Nonsmokers, on the other hand, consider the costs to outweigh the benefits, so they don't smoke. It's differences in tastes and preferences, not rationality or irrationality, that explain the different outcomes we observe.

MODERATOR: Are there other considerations that enter the process?

ECONOMIST: Yes. Differences in time preferences, for example. Some people attach a greater value to today while placing less importance on tomorrow. In technical terms, these are "present-oriented" people, who highly discount the future consequences of their current behavior. "Future-oriented" people, on the other hand, value the future more highly and attach greater weight to the utility—or disutility—of the adverse future consequences of actions taken today. Thus, the former would be more likely to smoke than the latter.

        Risk preferences also enter the picture. Remember, the adverse health consequences

of smoking do not afflict individuals with
absolute certainty. Instead, people are affected
according to some statistical chance of
suffering various smoking-related diseases.
Here, too, individuals can differ in terms of
their "taste" for accepting that risk. After all,
some people engage in skydiving and bungee
cord jumping, which are risky activities that
most of us choose to avoid. But that doesn't
mean they're behaving irrationally, given
their "taste" for risk. So those with a greater
tolerance for risk may take their chances and
smoke, while others who are more risk averse
will choose not to smoke.

ANTITOBACCO: That's all well and good, Professor, but it
                 seems to me that your theory ignores the
                 crucial fact that tobacco is *addictive*. People
                 may choose to smoke, but they don't choose
                 to be addicted. Isn't that incompatible with
                 your theory of rational, voluntary choice?

ECONOMIST: You raise a valid point, and I suspect many
                 economists would probably agree with you.

MODERATOR: I wonder if people really evaluate things in
                 such a cool, clinical, and analytical manner.
                 Regret, disappointment, lack of self-control,
                 overconfidence, compulsion—these seem to
                 be inherent aspects of everyday life, yet they
                 don't seem to fit your economic theory of
                 rational behavior.[33]

ECONOMIST: That, too, is a valid criticism. People do
                 sometimes act, not on the basis of detached
                 reason, but out of emotion, passion, and
                 egoism. In fact, a number of economists

recently have begun to incorporate these considerations into their theoretical analyses.[34] Other economists are attempting to integrate the findings from cognitive psychology into our economic thinking.[35]

PROTOBACCO: I think we're selling people short here. Some economists have formulated a theory of "rational addiction," which demonstrates that even addictive behavior represents rational, voluntary utility maximization over a longer-run time horizon.[36]

One economist who has studied smoking in great depth concludes that people do, in fact, behave rationally. He finds that smokers —including young smokers—are quite aware of the long-run health hazards of smoking, and that their behavior is consistent with their rationally taking these risks into account. In fact, he shows that smokers actually *overestimate* the true probability of contracting tobacco-related diseases as a result of all the screeching antismoking propaganda. A more accurate comprehension of the true risks, he calculates, would result in 8 percent *more* people smoking![37]

ANTITOBACCO: That particular theory, and the evidence underlying it, have been thoroughly discredited.[38]

The fact is that smoking is an addiction— it's not a free, rational choice. A Tobacco Institute memorandum of September 9, 1980, makes this crystal clear when it states: "We can't defend continued smoking as 'free choice' if the person was 'addicted'."[39]

Moreover, it is incomprehensible to me how consumer behavior can be characterized as "rational" when the industry has engaged in a decades-long campaign of deceptive marketing to confuse and mislead people about the dangers of smoking. Even writers for *The Wall Street Journal*—hardly a bastion of radicalism—describe the industry's conduct as "the longest-running misinformation campaign in U.S. business history."[40]

MODERATOR: Could you provide some examples to illustrate that claim?

ANTITOBACCO: I certainly can. First, consider the sheer volume and exponential growth of the industry's spending on advertising and promotion, as depicted in Graphic 2-4.

GRAPHIC 2-4

DOMESTIC CIGARETTE ADVERTISING AND PROMOTION EXPENDITURES
1973–1993

Year	Total*
1973	$ 247.5
1983	1,900.8
1993	6,035.4

*Total in millions of dollars.

Source: Federal Trade Commission, *Annual Report to Congress,* various years.

PROTOBACCO: It is an old, anticapitalist myth that advertising somehow brainwashes consumers into behaving in ways inimical to their own best interest. Advertising has a negligible influence in this respect.[41]

ANTITOBACCO: If that were true, then the managements of these firms would be guilty of wasting billions of their stockholders' funds on unproductive advertising activities. I don't believe that. And more important, neither do they.

MODERATOR: What do you mean?

ANTITOBACCO: The tobacco firms have deliberately misled, deceived, and confused people for decades about the dangers of smoking.

MODERATOR: I assume you have evidence to support that charge?

ANTITOBACCO: I certainly do. First, the industry's "research" organization, the Council on Tobacco Research, or CTR, has been a sham front for a massive disinformation campaign. Although framed in terms of "objective" scientific investigation of health and tobacco issues, in reality CTR has served as a propaganda machine for the purpose of sowing doubt about the medical dangers of tobacco— dangers that the firms' own researchers knew to be true.[42]

An industry trade group official described the firms' effort as a "brilliantly conceived and executed" strategy for "creating doubt about the health charge without actually denying it."[43]

Second, for decades the companies have devoted billions to persuade people that their products are not harmful, that their products are capable of protecting people's health—even that their products promote healthier living! They have invested billions to fabricate false auras of glamour, machismo, and adventurousness in order to seduce people into becoming addicted to their lethal products.

MODERATOR: Can you provide some examples?

ANTITOBACCO: Santa Claus declaring "Luckies are easy on my throat," slogans like "More doctors smoke Camels," and claims that "Viceroys give double-barrel health protection" are examples of promotional ploys used for decades by the industry to deceive people into believing that smoking was beneficial.[44]

As long ago as 1927, the American Tobacco Company advertised its Lucky Strikes by claiming that physicians recommend them as "less irritating to sensitive or tender throats," while Brown & Williamson promoted its Old Golds by fraudulently promising "not a cough in a carload."[45]

They've been doing this for decades, driving home their false message with billions in advertising expenditures.

PROTOBACCO: The industry merely discovered that health-oriented advertising was an effective method for promoting one firm's products over those of its rivals. By putting people's health concerns at the center of their marketing campaigns, a strong profit incentive arose for the tobacco companies to promote improvements in cigarette designs— especially during the "tar derby" of the late 1950s, when they reduced the tar content of their cigarettes by 60 percent.[46]

The overall results were beneficial. Consumers became better informed, became more aware and alert to health concerns about smoking, and were able to choose from a greater variety of safer cigarettes.

ANTITOBACCO: The companies were deceiving people into falsely believing there is such a thing as a "safe" cigarette when, of course, there isn't. Their purpose was to make their groundless claims believable.

Meanwhile, they were targeting young people generally, and young women in particular, in order to create new addicts to replace the hundreds of thousands of older ones who die from smoking each year.[47] So they devised Joe Camel to appeal to children as young as 12 and 13, and came up with the Virginia Slims "You've come a long way, baby" campaign to hook young women.[48]

A 1969 marketing report to the board of directors of Philip Morris attests to the persuasive power of tobacco companies' youth promotional campaigns. Pointedly noting that the first smoke is "a noxious experience," the report stresses that youth marketing must initially emphasize smoking as an appealing and symbolic act of adolescent defiance. "As the force from the psychological symbolism subsides," it points out, "the pharmacological effect takes over to sustain the habit."[49]

I don't see how it could be stated any clearer than that: Smoking is *not* something individuals would rationally choose to do on their own, but once marketing campaigns successfully entice them into trying it, they're hooked!

PROTOBACCO: Lower-level marketing types get carried away in their enthusiasm and hyperbole. The chief executive officers of the tobacco companies have denied under oath that their firms engaged in any marketing efforts directed at underage young people.[50]

ANTITOBACCO: These are not documents prepared by low-level operatives. These are documents prepared under the auspices of high-ranking senior officials of the firms.[51] And their denials expose them to perjury proceedings.

MODERATOR: Are there any other ways in which you think the companies have deceived or misled consumers?

ANTITOBACCO: Yes. Although the firms' marketing and package labeling assure consumers about lower tar levels in cigarettes, the companies secretly have been engineering *greater* amounts of nicotine into their products in order to "spike" them and enhance their addictiveness.[52]

PROTOBACCO: Another unsubstantiated charge that tobacco companies have denied. They have tried but failed to duplicate FDA Commissioner Kessler's charts purporting to show a diverging trend between tar and nicotine in their products.[53]

ANTITOBACCO: Indisputable is the fact that the companies have undertaken research to develop genetically altered tobacco plants capable of delivering more nicotine than conventional flue-cured tobacco.[54] And they have done so knowing full well, as a 1982 Brown & Williamson document explains, "Once addiction takes place, it becomes necessary for the smoker to make peace with the accepted hazards. This is done by a wide range of rationalizations."[55]

The companies deliberately kept the public in the dark about what they secretly knew to be true. Brown & Williamson admitted that "very few customers are aware of the effects of nicotine, i.e., its addictive nature, and that nicotine is a poison."[56] An R. J. Reynolds survey, for example, found that smokers had no idea what the tar and nicotine numbers meant on their cigarette warning labels.[57]

Little wonder that Judge Sarokin wrote in his legal decision against the firms that "the tobacco industry may be the king of concealment and disinformation."[58] How anyone can construe tobacco consumption as "rational," utility-maximizing behavior in the face of this overwhelming evidence to the contrary simply defies comprehension.

PROTOBACCO: Judge Sarokin's biased remarks resulted in his being removed from the case by the Third Circuit Court of Appeals.[59]

MODERATOR: Professor, can economic theory resolve these conflicting claims concerning the industry's marketing campaigns?

ECONOMIST: Yes and no.

MODERATOR: Spoken like a true economist! Please explain.

ECONOMIST: Yes, if people act on the basis of incorrect or deceptive information, then one cannot reasonably conclude that their behavior rationally advances their well-being.

    However, when it comes to the impact of advertising more generally, I'm afraid no definitive answer is available. Arguments about this have raged in the economics profession for a long time, with no clear-cut resolution in sight.[60]

MODERATOR: I think we've reached an impasse here.

ECONOMIST: But we needn't get bogged down. After all, it is what economists call the "price elasticity of demand" that captures the essence of consumer behavior in this respect.

MODERATOR: Any port will do in a storm! Why don't you explain that and let's see if we can make some headway.

ECONOMIST: All right. Let me divide it into two parts: "demand" and then the "elasticity" of that demand.

The demand for something is how much of it people are willing to buy at various prices—holding constant their income as well as their tastes and preferences. It's an expression of preferences that stems from the utility maximization theory of rational consumer behavior we've just discussed.

MODERATOR: How would addiction enter the picture?

ECONOMIST: Through what economists call the "price elasticity of demand." You see, price elasticity measures how sensitive buyers are to *changes* in the price of something.

An "elastic" demand for something means that a 10 percent increase in the price will result in a more than 10 percent drop in the quantity of the good demanded. In technical terms, the price elasticity of demand is greater than one, and buyers are said to be relatively sensitive to price.

On the other hand, an "inelastic" demand means the opposite—that buyers are relatively insensitive to changes in the price of a good. In other words, a 10 percent increase in the price would result in a less than 10 percent decline in the quantity demanded. In this case, the price elasticity of demand would have a value less than one, and the demand would be classified as inelastic.

MODERATOR: In the case of cigarettes, can you provide us any estimates for the price elasticity of demand?

ECONOMIST: Yes. In its latest report, the Federal Trade Commission[61] accepts an estimate of –0.4. In other words, a 10 percent increase in the price of cigarettes will be accompanied by a 4 percent decline in cigarette consumption.

MODERATOR: So the demand is inelastic?

ECONOMIST: That's right.

MODERATOR: What's the basis for the commission's estimate?

ECONOMIST: The commission cites a host of econometric studies that report elasticity estimates in the range of –0.2 to –0.8.[62] This figure also represents the midpoint of the consensus range of elasticity estimates arrived at by a gathering of economists and other experts convened by the National Cancer Institute. The estimates at that conference ranged from –0.3 to –0.5. There was no disagreement as to the highly inelastic nature of cigarette demand.[63] Moreover, the most recent industry data suggest an elasticity of –0.3.[64]

PROTOBACCO: That's true. But all the studies you've cited rely on historical data to measure elasticity and generally derive estimates based on "short-run" or immediate impacts of a price change. Every student of economics principles knows that demand responds more to a price change the longer the time period over which consumer reaction is measured.

ECONOMIST: Your point is well taken . . .

PROTOBACCO: I'm sure you're aware of studies that have attempted to measure the "long-run" elasticity of demand. One such study was done by Professor Gary Becker of the University of Chicago—a winner of the Nobel Prize in economics. He found that the long-run response to a permanent change in cigarette prices falls between –0.73 and –0.79, with an average estimate of –0.75. His findings imply that a 10 percent increase in the price of cigarettes will cause a short-run decline in sales of approximately 4 percent but a longer-run decline in demand of 7.5 percent.[65]

ECONOMIST: I agree that, over time, as prices escalate to unprecedented levels, consumer sensitivity to price increases becomes more pronounced and that demand therefore becomes less inelastic.

PROTOBACCO: That's certainly the finding of a study by the Congressional Research Service. It implies that the long-run elasticity of demand for cigarettes could be as high as –1.2. By this measure, the demand is elastic: a 10 percent rise in price would result in a long-run decline in cigarette sales of 12 percent.[66]

ECONOMIST: I consider that estimate exaggerated, but I recognize that it is difficult to predict long-run consequences with any exact degree of precision. What is relevant for public policy, however, are the elasticity numbers that confront us here and now.

MODERATOR: If that's the case, what should government policymakers keep in mind?

ECONOMIST: Three things. First, by any measure the demand for cigarettes is substantially inelastic. This means that the price of cigarettes will have to be increased by a very large amount if it is to be an effective tool in curbing cigarette consumption.

Second, this inelasticity of demand also explains why cigarette production is very profitable. Every price increase outweighs the decline in demand that follows and thus can enhance the firms' revenues. Consequently, a mandated price increase, without more, will simply put more profits in the tobacco companies' pockets.

Third, the elasticity of demand is different for different smoking populations, so the impact of a policy of higher prices will also differ accordingly.

MODERATOR: What do you mean?

ECONOMIST: Teenagers, for example, have a higher demand elasticity for cigarettes than smokers generally—by some tobacco company estimates, an elasticity of –1.2— which means that a 10 percent increase in the price of cigarettes would lead to a decline of 12 percent in the number of teenagers who would begin to smoke.[67]

To indicate the significance of this, the Philip Morris Company calculated that the 1982–1983 round of cigarette price increases prevented some 600,000 teenagers from starting to smoke.[68]

MODERATOR: Why are teenagers so much more responsive to price changes?

ECONOMIST: Perhaps because they have less money to spend than adults. Perhaps, also, because they're not yet as strongly habituated to nicotine as those who've been smoking longer. As a result, they are more sensitive to price changes than adults.

MODERATOR: What are the implications of these findings for public policy?

ECONOMIST: If the president's goal of reducing teenage smoking by 60 percent over the next decade is going to be met, cigarette prices will have to be increased by a large amount—at the very least by $1.50 per pack.

PROTOBACCO: I think it's naive to presume that the government, or the tobacco industry, or anybody else for that matter, can control the social behavior of young people. Teenagers will be teenagers: the more hazardous you make smoking appear, the more you enhance its appeal to them.

ANTITOBACCO: Given that about 80 percent of smokers take up the habit before age 18, the benefits of any reduction in teen smoking would be magnified greatly over the long run.

ECONOMIST: I don't mean to minimize the difficulty of the task. The demand for cigarettes is stubbornly inelastic—not only in the United States but worldwide.

MODERATOR: Can you provide us some evidence of that?

ECONOMIST: Take the case of the Netherlands, for example. As Graphic 2-5 demonstrates, cigarette prices in Holland escalated by more than 70 percent between 1988 and 1996. Yet cigarette consumption did not decrease. In fact, it actually went up![69]

MODERATOR: That's inelasticity ne plus ultra!

ECONOMIST: We must be careful, however, not to jump to conclusions on the basis of international or intercultural comparisons. Social customs and habits are not the same everywhere. Despite hefty tobacco prices, youth smoking rates

GRAPHIC 2-5

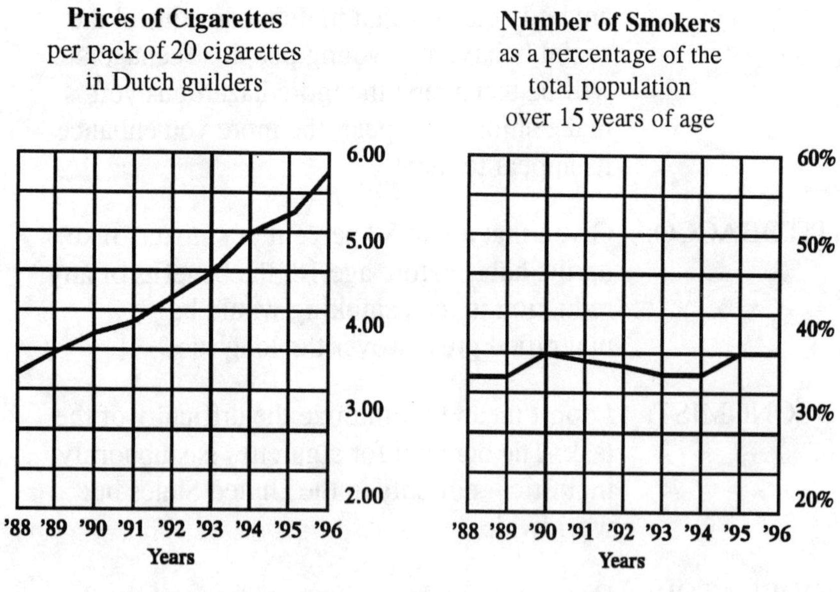

Prices of Cigarettes
per pack of 20 cigarettes
in Dutch guilders

Number of Smokers
as a percentage of the
total population
over 15 years of age

Source: Stichting Rokers Belangen (Dutch Smokers Alliance), 1997.

have remained stubbornly high in Britain and Scandinavia. Yet, when Canadian cigarette taxes were raised from 42¢ to $1.93 between 1984 and 1992, youth smoking rates fell by 60 percent.

MODERATOR: Perhaps we can conclude, then, by recognizing that smoking is influenced by a variety of factors: price, price gaps, availability of substitute products, demographics, inflation, consumer income, social and cultural attitudes, smoking regulations, and so forth. Moreover, many of these parameters are subject to considerable uncertainty in the future and will be significantly impacted by public policies now under consideration.

ECONOMIST: That's a fair summary. But let's remember that all these factors and influences are taken into account in estimating the elasticity of demand for cigarettes, and the data show that this demand is highly inelastic—that smokers respond very little to price changes and price increases.

PROTOBACCO: Let us also remember that this is a free enterprise economy in which people are free to choose how to dispose of their income and free to do as they please.

ANTITOBACCO: Do you mean that people are free to sell heroin to grade-school children at playgrounds? That thieves are free to mug people in order to enhance the "disposable income" available to them for spending? Or that scam artists are free to fleece the elderly? I still find a great deal of this discussion weirdly surrealistic. Tobacco companies and their propagandists always wrap their arguments in an appeal to people's "freedom to choose." But, to repeat once more, if tobacco is addictive, then are smokers really free to choose? Or are they slaves to an uncontrollable vice?

MODERATOR: That's an excellent question. I want to thank our guests for making this a lively and informative evening. And I invite our viewers back next week, when we tackle the issue of competition and monopoly in "The Tobacco Wars."

REFERENCES

[1] Centers for Disease Control, *1995 National Household Survey on Drug Abuse* (Washington, DC: GPO, August 1996).

[2] Ibid.

[3] Ibid.

[4] U.S. Centers for Disease Control, "Tobacco Use Among U.S. Racial/Ethnic Minority Groups," news release, April 27, 1998.

[5] U.S. Department of Health and Human Services, *The Health Consequences of Smoking for Women: A Report of the Surgeon General,* Public Health Service, Office on Smoking and Health (Washington, DC: GPO, 1980), pp. 37-38.

[6] National Institutes of Health, "Risks of Cigarette Smoking for Women on the Rise," press release, Apr. 23, 1997.

[7] Jane E. Brody, "A Fatal Shift in Cancer's Gender Gap," *New York Times,* May 12, 1998, p. B13.

[8] Centers for Disease Control, *1995 National Survey.*

[9] C. Everett Koop, "Don't Forget the Smokers," *Washington Post* (national weekly ed.), Mar. 16, 1998, p. 27.

[10] Centers for Disease Control, *1995 National Survey.* See also U.S. Department of Health and Human Services, *Preventing Tobacco Use Among Young People*, Centers for Disease Control and Prevention, Office on Smoking and Health, July 1994.

[11] U.S. Food and Drug Administration, Proposed Rule, Regulations Restricting the Sale and Distribution of Cigarettes and Smokeless Tobacco Products to Protect Children and Adolescents, 60 *Federal Register,* (Aug. 11, 1995), p. 41314.

[12] U.S. Food and Drug Administration, "Children and Tobacco: The Facts," press release, Aug. 10, 1995.

[13] World Health Organization, *The Tobacco Epidemic: A Global Health Emergency* (1997).

[14] Ibid.

[15] Ibid.

[16] Lorraine Mooney, "The WHO's Misplaced Priorities," *The Wall Street Journal Europe,* Aug. 25, 1997.

[17] State of Minnesota v. Philip Morris Inc., Haas Letter, May 27, 1970, (Blilely papers, document LG 2002660).

[18] Hans J. Eysenck, "Smoking and Health," in *Smoking and Society,* Robert D. Tollison, ed. (Lexington, MA: Lexington Books, 1986), pp. 20-21.

[19] Centers for Disease Control and Prevention, *Mortality and Morbidity Weekly Report*, 1993; 42: 645–49.

[20] U.S. Department of Health and Human Services, National Center for Health Statistics, *Vital Statistics of the United States,* (Hyattsville, MD: 1996), Tables 1-1, 1-23.

[21] T. D. Sterling, W. L. Rosenbaum, and J. J. Weinkam, "Risk Attribution and Tobacco-Related Deaths," 138 *American Journal of Epidemiology* (1993): 132.

[22] Centers for Disease Control, *1995 National Survey.* See also K. E. Warner, M. T. Halpern and G. A. Giovino, "Differences by Education in Smoker/Non-Smoker Beliefs About the Dangers of Smoking," 9 *Health Education Research,* (1994), pp. 139–43.

[23] Sherwin J. Feinhandler, "The Social Role of Smoking," in *Smoking and Society*, ed. Robert D. Tollison, (Lexington, MA: Lexington Books, 1986), p. 183.

[24] Charles D. Spielberger, "Psychological Determinants of Smoking Behavior," in *Smoking and Society*; State of Minnesota v. Philip Morris, Inc., "Smoker Psychology Research: Presentation to Philip Morris Board of Directors," Dr. H. Wakeham, Nov. 26, 1969 (Trial Exhibit No. 10,229); State of Minnesota v. Philip Morris, Inc., "Motives and Incentives in Cigarette Smoking," William L. Dunn, Philip Morris Company, undated (Trial Exhibit No. 18,089); Robert D. Tollison and Richard E. Wagner, *The Economics of Smoking* (Boston: Kluwer Academic Publishers, 1992), p. 188.

[25] State of Minnesota v. Philip Morris, Inc., "Motives and Incentives in Cigarette Smoking," William L. Dunn, Philip Morris Research Center, undated (Trial Exhibit No. 18,089).

[26] State of Minnesota v. Philip Morris, Inc., Research Planning Memorandum on the Nature of the Tobacco Business and the Crucial Role of Nicotine Therein, Claude E. Teague, Jr., Apr. 14, 1972 (Trial Exhibit No. 12,408).

[27] U.S. Department of Health and Human Services, *Smoking and Health in the Americas: A 1992 Report of the Surgeon General in Collaboration with the Pan American Health Organization,* Public Health Service, Office on Smoking and Health, 1992, p. 17.

[28] Ibid., p. 20.

[29] Feinhandler, "The Social Role of Smoking," p. 171.

[30] Jeremy Bentham, *Principles of Morals and Legislation,* Chap. 1, "Of the Principle of Utility," reprinted in *The Varieties of Economics*, ed. Robert Lekachman (Gloucester, Mass.: Peter Smith, 1977), p. 203.

[31] Ibid., p. 204.

[32] *Smoking and Health: A Report of the Surgeon General,* U.S. Department of Health, Education, and Welfare, Public Health Service, Office on Smoking and Health, 1979, pp. A6-A8.

[33] See "Rational Economic Man," *The Economist,* Dec. 24, 1994, pp. 90–92.

[34] See Matthew Rabin, "Psychology and Economics," 36 *Journal of Economic Literature* (Mar. 1998): 11–46; Jon Elster, "Emotions and Economic Theory," 36 *Journal of Economic Literature* (Mar. 1998): 47–74; Robert H. Frank, *Passions Within Reason* (New York: Norton, 1988); Richard H. Thaler, *The Winner's Curse: Paradoxes and Anomalies of Economic Life* (New York: Free Press, 1992). For an early pathbreaking critique, see Amartya Sen, "Rational Fools: A Critique of the Behavioral Foundations of Economic Theory," 6 *Philosophy and Public Affairs* (1977): 317–344.

[35] See George A. Ackerlof, "Procrastination and Obedience," 81 *American Economic Review* (May 1991), pp. 1–19.

[36] Gary S. Becker and Kevin M. Murphy, "A Theory of Rational Addiction," 96 *Journal of Political Economy* (Aug. 1988), pp. 675–700.

[37] W. Kip Viscusi, *Smoking: Making the Risky Decision* (New York: Oxford University Press, 1992).

[38] Jon D. Hanson and Kyle D. Logue, "The Costs of Cigarettes: The Economic Case for Ex Post Incentive-Based Regulation," 107 *Yale Law Journal* (1998): 1186–1223.

[39] State of Minnesota v. Philip Morris Inc., Knopick Memorandum, Sept. 9, 1980 (Trial Exhibit No. 14,303).

[40] Alix M. Freedman and Laurie P. Cohen, "How Cigarette Makers Keep Health Question 'Open' Year After Year," *The Wall Street Journal,* Feb. 11, 1993, p. 1.

[41] Robert D. Tollison and Richard E. Wagner, *The Economics of Smoking* (Boston: Kluwer Academic Publishers, 1992), pp. 146–47.

[42] Freedman and Cohen, "Cigarette Makers."

[43] Panzer Memorandum, Tobacco Institute, May 1, 1972. Cited in Complaint, State of Maryland v. Philip Morris Inc., Baltimore City Circuit Court, Case No. 86122017/CL211487, June 16, 1997, p. 10.

[44] Cited in Complaint, State of Texas v. American Tobacco Co., U.S. District Court, Eastern District of Texas, June 16, 1997.

[45] American Heart Association et al., Petition Before the Food and Drug Administration, Apr. 25, 1988, p. 12 (reprinted in U.S. Congress. House. Subcommittee on Health and the Environment. *Regulation of Tobacco Products, part 1: Hearing Before the Subcommittee on Health and the Environment,* 103d Cong., 2d sess., 1995, p.243.

[46] John E. Calfee, "The Ghost of Cigarette Advertising Past," *Regulation,* (summer 1997), pp. 38, 44.

[47] See Barry Meier, "Files of R. J. Reynolds Tobacco Show Effort on Youths," *New York Times,* Jan. 15, 1998, p. A10.

[48] State of Minnesota v. Philip Morris Inc., "Incidence of Smoking Cigarettes," Philip Morris Co., May 18, 1973, Trial Exhibit No. 3072.

[49] State of Minnesota v. Philip Morris Inc., Draft of Annual Report to Philip Morris Board by Vice President for Research and Development, Fall 1969 (Trial Exhibit No. 3681).

[50] Meier, "Files of R. J. Reynolds." Jan. 15, 1998.

[51] Letter from Congressman Henry Waxman to Congressman Thomas Blilely, Chair, Committee on Commerce, U.S. House of Representatives, Jan. 14, 1998.

[52] House Subcommittee, *Regulation of Tobacco Products, part 1,* pp. 121–26 (testimony of Dr. David A. Kessler, Commissioner, Food and Drug Administration); *Congressional Record,* House, July 31, 1995 (submission by Congressman Henry Waxman); Barry Meier, "Cigarette Maker Manipulated Nicotine, Its Records Suggest," *New York Times,* Feb. 23, 1998, p. 1.

[53] House Subcommittee, *Regulation of Tobacco Products, part 1,* p. 577 (statement of R. J. Reynolds Tobacco Company); Meier, "Cigarette Maker."

[54] Milo Geyelin, "Tobacco Executive Expects a Subpoena," *The Wall Street Journal,* Feb. 20, 1998, p. B5.

[55] *ASH* Web site, Conyers documents release. On youth advertising more generally, see Environmental Protection Agency, "Proposed Rule: Regulations Restricting the Sale and Distribution of Cigarettes and Smokeless Tobacco Products to Protect Children and Adolescents," 60 *Federal Register,* No. 155 (Aug. 11, 1995), pp. 41328-34.

[56] State of Minnesota v. Philip Morris Inc., Steele Memorandum, Aug. 24, 1978, Trial Exhibit No. 13,677.

[57] State of Minnesota v. Philip Morris Inc., " 'Tar' and Nicotine Awareness and Attitude Study," R. J. Reynolds, Oct. 1975, Trial Exhibit No. 12,484.

[58] Haines v. Liggett Group, Inc., 140 F.R.D. 681 (D. N.J. 1992).

[59] Haines v. Liggett Group, Inc., 975 F.2d 81 (3d Cir. 1992).

[60] See the exchange between John Kenneth Galbraith and others, "Time and the New Industrial State," 78 *American Economic Review,* (May 1988): 373–82.

[61] Federal Trade Commission, "Competition and the Financial Impact of the Proposed Tobacco Industry Settlement," (Washington, DC: GPO, Sept. 1997).

[62] See Congressional Budget Office, "The Proposed Tobacco Settlement: Issues from a Federal Perspective," April 1998; F. Chaloupka and M. Grossman, *Price, Tobacco Control Policies and Youth Smoking,* National Bureau of Economic Research, Working Paper No. 5740, 1996; and U.S. Department of Health and Human Services, *Preventing Tobacco Use Among Young People,* 1994.

[63] National Cancer Institute, National Institutes of Health, *The Impact of Cigarette Excise Taxes on Smoking Among Children and Adults: Summary of a National Cancer Institute Expert Panel,* 1993.

[64] Suein L. Hwang, "Philip Morris Posts a 2% Drop in Quarterly Net." *The Wall Street Journal,* July 22, 1998, p. A4.

[65] Becker, Gary S. et al., "Analysis of Cigarette Addiction," 84 *American Economic Review,* (June 1994), p. 407.

[66] Jane G. Gravelle and Dennis Zimmerman, *Taxes to Fund Health Care Reform: An Economic Analysis,* Congressional Research Service, Library of Congress, Mar. 8, 1994.

[67] State of Minnesota v. Philip Morris Inc., "Teenage Smoking and the Federal Excise Tax on Cigarettes," Philip Morris, Sept. 17, 1981, Trial Exhibit No. 10,560.

[68] State of Minnesota v. Philip Morris Inc., "Handling an Excise Tax Increase," Philip Morris, Sept. 3, 1987, Trial Ex. No. 11,591.

III. The Antitrust Front

MODERATOR: Welcome, ladies and gentlemen, to the third
in our series of programs on the tobacco wars.
Our subject tonight is the issue of competition
and monopoly in the U.S. tobacco industry
and the near century-long litigation of this
industry under the antitrust laws.

It is probably superfluous to remind our
viewers that in our free enterprise society the
basic organizing principle is the competitive
market. It is at once a mechanism for allocating
society's scarce resources—deciding what
goods to produce, in what quantities, and by
what techniques—and a regulatory mechanism
for controlling private power.

Like the political framework prescribed
by the Constitution, competition rests upon
distrust of concentrated power and upon a
belief in the maximum possible diffusion of
rights and opportunities. Decision-making
power over such vital matters as price,
production, and investment is to be widely
decentralized among many firms, not
concentrated in one or a handful. While
private enterprisers are free to assume the
responsibility and exercise the power of
organizing the productive activities on which
the life of the community depends, they have
to pay a price for that freedom: they have to
submit to the discipline of competition. They
have to obey the dictates of the market instead
of dictating to it. They have to heed the voice
of the community (as expressed in the
market) rather than serving it only as they

deem fit and proper. In short, society grants individuals the privilege of economic freedom only because competition imposes the checks and balances to constrain that freedom in the public interest.

One further aspect of competition should be noted. ~~As long as the market functions effectively in controlling private power, there is no need for massive government intervention to protect society from economic exploitation.~~ To the extent, therefore, that business accepts the constraints and discipline of competition, it avoids the direct government regulation characteristic of command-and-control economies.

With this background in mind, let us turn to the question of competition and monopoly in the tobacco industry. To discuss this subject, we are fortunate to have two nationally preeminent experts in the antitrust field. One is a distinguished professor of antitrust economics at a major research university; the other is a leading antitrust attorney who has represented the tobacco industry both in state and federal courts. Professor?

ECONOMIST: Well, as you know, the first landmark case against the tobacco industry was filed early in the 20th century. At the time, the public was alarmed by the proliferation of combinations and trusts that had come to dominate major sectors of American industry. The suit against the tobacco trust, like the companion suit against the oil trust, accused the defendants of monopolizing their respective industries in violation of the Sherman Antitrust Act of 1890.

In the case of tobacco, the Justice Department accused the trust of achieving a near-90 percent control of all the major segments of the industry—with the notable exception of large cigars. Graphic 3-1 illustrates the market control achieved by the trust.

GRAPHIC 3-1

TRUST'S SHARE OF TOBACCO PRODUCTS

Year	Plug	Smoking	Fine Cut	Snuff	Cigarettes	Little Cigars
1891	2.7%	18.0%	3.3%	3.6%	88.9%	
1892	3.5	21.9	4.1	4.0	87.9	
1893	5.9	21.7	4.7	4.7	85.3	
1894	5.6	20.6	4.3	3.4	86.5	
1895	12.4	22.5	4.3	3.9	87.3	
1896	20.1	20.7	4.5	5.6	83.4	
1897	20.9	22.7	4.6	4.8	80.0	
1898	23.0	26.9	6.0	6.1	88.3	48.7%
1899	56.3	54.3	48.5	32.4	94.7	54.7
1900	62.0	59.2	50.5	78.0	92.7	60.6
1901	67.7	57.8	48.1	80.2	89.9	73.3
1902	71.2	66.3	73.7	85.9	84.6	71.8
1903	76.9	67.1	77.6	89.4	83.9	67.9
1904	78.2	69.2	80.4	90.6	87.7	79.2
1905	80.7	68.7	81.7	93.8	84.7	78.3
1906	81.8	70.6	80.9	96.0	82.5	81.3
1907	80.5	72.4	81.4	95.7	81.7	90.8
1908	81.9	73.6	79.2	95.7	81.8	88.7
1909	83.3	75.3	80.1	96.1	83.6	89.0
1910	84.9	76.2	79.7	96.5	86.1	91.4

Source: Henry R. Seager & Charles A. Gulick, Jr., *Trust and Corporation Problems* (New York: Harper & Bros., 1929), p. 163.

This, said the Justice Department, was tantamount to monopoly and, therefore, a violation of the law.

ATTORNEY: The facts, as you state them, are correct, but the implication is misleading.

MODERATOR: Why?

ATTORNEY: The genesis of the tobacco trust, as well as other trusts of the time, was not rooted in monopoly. It merely reflected the battle for survival of the fittest. The real function of these trusts was to promote efficiency and to get rid of weak entrepreneurs.

MODERATOR: Would you elaborate?

ATTORNEY: I think old John D. Rockefeller, who organized the Standard Oil trust, put it best. He pointed out that the growth of giant corporations was nothing more than the victory of the most deserving producers in the competitive market place. "The American Beauty rose," he said, "can be produced in the splendor and fragrance which bring cheer to its beholder only by sacrificing the early buds which grow up around it. This is not an evil tendency in business. It is merely the working out of a law of nature and a law of God."[1]

ECONOMIST: That's great purple prose, but clearly at odds with the facts. If you would reread the Supreme Court's 1911 decision, you would find that the trust did not achieve its overwhelming market control by superior efficiency but by resort to predatory tactics designed to destroy competition.[2]

MODERATOR: Such as . . .

ECONOMIST: One was geographical price discrimination. The trust used the immense profits from its early monopoly in cigarettes to subsidize price wars—first in one region, then another, first in one product, then another—until competition was brought to its knees. The trust's overpowering financial resources were at once the bludgeon by which competitors were subdued and the net by which they were drawn to sell out to the trust.

The trust used this tactic with devastating effectiveness during the "plug war" that started in 1893. Once the trust had decided to gain control of this segment of the industry, it slashed prices by as much as 70 percent, willingly incurring losses on its sales below cost. In addition, it used fighting brands—one of which was appropriately named "Battle Axe"—as an instrument for destroying competition. These fighting brands were given away by the hundred-weight during the plug war but they served the purpose for which they were intended.

Graphic 3-2 tells the story. The trust's losses from its plug operations escalated from $215,000 in 1893 to a peak of $1.4 million in 1896, and totaled $4 million over the duration of the plug war. At the time, this was a substantial sum compared to companywide profits of approximately $15 million over the same period.

GRAPHIC 3-2

PREDATION DURING THE PLUG WAR

Year	Trust Share of Plug Market (%)	Trust Profits/(Losses) Plug Market	Companywide Trust Profits
1893	5.9	$ (215,000)	$ 4,334,000
1894	5.6	110,000	5,065,000
1895	12.4	(913,000)	3,817,000
1896	20.1	(1,378,000)	3,413,000
1897	20.9	(890,000)	3,996,000
1898	23.0	(942,000)	3,585,000
1899	56.3	1,930,000	6,709,000
1900	62.0	4,222,000	10,433,000
1901	67.7	7,714,000	15,077,000
1902	71.2	11,123,000	16,891,000
1903	76.9	12,952,000	

Source: Department of Commerce and Labor, *Report of the Commissioner of Corporations on the Tobacco Industry* (1909), Part I, p. 365; Part III (1915), p. 51; Henry R. Seager & Charles A. Gulick, Jr., *Trust and Corporation Problems* (New York: Harper & Bros., 1929), p. 169.

Obviously, unlike its smaller victims, the trust could offset its losses in plug with profits drawn from other, monopolized products and regions. At each step of the way it was also able to limit its losses to the product and region currently under attack until they too were swept clean of competitors. It was a strategy that worked to perfection, not only in plug but also in snuff and other products. The only exception was large cigars that—unlike cigarettes—could not be mass produced by machine.

MODERATOR: Any other trust tactics that were used in its monopolization campaign?

ECONOMIST: Throughout its history, the trust made it a practice to buy up competitors whose business had become successful. Many of these acquisitions were made secretly and the trust's control concealed. The trust continued to operate them as "bogus" independents— thereby appealing to antitrust and pro-union sentiment in the country—and often used them as a special weapon to attack the business of genuine competitors.

Also, many other firms were purchased at great expense only to be closed down—the purchase agreement generally stipulating that the sellers would refrain from competition far into the future.

MODERATOR: And so the Supreme Court in 1911 found that the trust had illegally monopolized the tobacco industry and ordered its dissolution?

ECONOMIST: Yes. In the cigarette branch of the industry, the court created four successor companies that have survived to the present day: Liggett & Myers, Lorillard, Reynolds, and a new American Tobacco Co.

MODERATOR: Did this usher in a new era of competition in the industry?

ECONOMIST: Not quite. It created an oligopoly—what
Louis Brandeis warned would be "four
monopolies instead of one."

MODERATOR: Was the Brandeis prophecy correct?

ECONOMIST: To a large extent. Look at Graphic 3-3. Three-
quarters of a century after the dissolution
decree, the top four cigarette producers still
collectively dominate 98 percent of cigarette
sales in the United States.[3]

ATTORNEY: Those numbers are highly misleading. The
collective market shares you cite may have
remained relatively stable over the years, but
those of individual companies have fluctuated
wildly. Leadership in the industry is subject to
constant change. At one time, Liggett was the
top firm in the business. Today, Philip Morris
—a company that didn't even exist in 1911—
has roughly 50 percent, and Liggett is down
to less than 2 percent. This shows just how
competitive the industry is and how slippery
the slope is at the top.

MODERATOR: Perhaps our economist can explain how
economic theory can contribute to our
understanding of the industry.

ECONOMIST: The cigarette industry is a classic, tight-knit
oligopoly, securely insulated from challenge
by new entry. Conscious parallel action, price
leadership, and price followership are the
order of the day. There is no price

GRAPHIC 3-3

CIGARETTES: COMPANY SHARES
AND MARKET CONCENTRATION

	1910	1925	1934	1953	1980	1995
American Tobacco Co.	37%	21%	26%	33%	11%	[d]
Liggett & Myers	28	27	27	17	2	2
Lorillard	15	2	4	7	10	8
R. J. Reynolds	0	42	26	26	33	26
Philip Morris Co.	[a]	1	2	10	31	46
Brown & Williamson	[b]	[b]	8	7	14	18
Share of Top Four Firms[c]:	80%	92%	87%	86%	89%	98%

[a] Less than 0.5%.
[b] Not available.
[c] Share of top three firms for 1910.
[d] American acquired by Brown & Williamson; sales contained in Brown & Williamson market share.

Sources: William H. Nicholls, *Price Policies in the Cigarette Industry* (Nashville: Vanderbilt University Press, 1951), Tables 9, 24; Simon N. Whitney, *Antitrust Policies*, vol. 2 (New York: Twentieth Century Fund, 1958), p. 25; Richard B. Tennant, *The American Cigarette Industry* (New Haven, CT: Yale University Press, 1950), Table 19; *American Tobacco Co. v. United States*, 328 U.S. 781, 794 (1946); *Business Week*, Jan. 8, 1955, p. 58; William B. Burnett, "Predation by a Nondominant Firm: The Liggett Case," in *The Antitrust Revolution*, ed. J. Kwoka & L. White (New York: Harper Collins College Publishers, 1994), Table 10-2; *Standard & Poor's*, "Industry Survey: Alcoholic Beverages & Tobacco," Jan. 23, 1997, p. 5.

competition—except on the rarest of occasions. Even without explicit agreements among the oligopolists, they operate like a cartel.

MODERATOR: Could you illustrate how this works in the cigarette industry?

ECONOMIST: ~~The coordinated implementation of the 1980 price increase is typical of the congenial and~~ nonaggressive behavior by the firms in this industry. As Graphic 3-4 shows, Reynolds led the increase, and its fellow oligopolists dutifully followed. Within less than a week, the industry had successfully engineered a general price increase—without dissent or deviation by any one of its member firms.

ATTORNEY: That's a single incident. It lacks statistical significance. It doesn't prove anything. Besides, it's ancient history.

ECONOMIST: On the contrary. It reflects the modus operandi—the way of life—in this industry ever since the dissolution of the trust. Back in the 1920s, there were only three changes in the industry's uniform price structure. Each price change was dutifully embraced by each of the oligopolists within a period of one to five days. Significantly, the Reynolds price increase at the height of the Great Depression —certainly one of the most difficult to explain in the nation's history—was followed within 24 hours by the other successor companies of the old trust.

GRAPHIC 3-4

CIGARETTE LIST PRICE INCREASES

	Announcement Date	85 mm cigarettes		100 mm cigarettes	
		Price Before	Price After	Price Before	Price After
Reynolds	May 2	$17.05	$17.65	$17.55	$18.15
American	May 5	17.05	17.65	17.55	18.15
Lorillard	May 5	17.05	17.65	17.55	18.15
Liggett	May 6	17.05	17.65	17.55	18.15
Brown & Williamson	May 7	17.05	17.65	17.55	18.15
Philip Morris	May 8	17.05	17.65	17.55	18.15

Source: William B. Burnett, *Predation by a Nondominant Firm: The* Liggett *Case*, in *The Antitrust Revolution* 2d ed., ed. J. Kwoka & L. White (New York: Harper Collins College Publishers, 1994), p. 224, Table 10-2.

More recently, in the 1980s and 1990s, the same pattern prevailed. Branded cigarette prices were raised by each of the oligopolists by identical amounts—from $4.04 per carton in January 1982 to $9.23 in June 1989, and to $13.25 in July 1992.[4] This impressive 228 percent increase over the period was dubbed by *The Wall Street Journal* as "one of the great magic tricks of market economics: how to force prices up and increase profits in an industry in which demand falls by tens of billions of cigarettes each year."[5]

ATTORNEY: Such firm behavior reflects nothing more than oligopolistic rationality—the profit-maximizing conduct of firms in a highly concentrated industry. They may not be aware of it, but the firms instinctively follow Henry Wadsworth Longfellow's admonition:

> "All your strength is your union.
> All your danger is in discord;
> Therefore be at peace henceforth,
> And as brothers live together."

What else do you expect?

ECONOMIST: What you call "oligopolistic rationality" really is tacit collusion. The outcome is the same as if the oligopolists had sat around the table in some remote hunting lodge and agreed on the price that all of them would charge on a date certain. In this case, whether collusion is tacit or overt, the results are the same: a noncompetitive price yielding supracompetitive profits.

ATTORNEY: It is strange that I am put in the position of having to explain oligopolistic rationality to an economist. As you well know, in an industry dominated by the so-called Big Three or Big Four, each firm will—quite rationally—recognize the fact of mutual interdependence.

MODERATOR: Which means . . .

ATTORNEY: It means that in an oligopoly situation a firm contemplating a price increase knows that each of its rivals will understand its common interest in following that increase. The other firms will understand that if they do not follow quickly, the lead firm will be compelled to lower its price to the previous level; ~~if they do follow, all will enjoy the benefits of the higher price and probably, if the demand for the product is inelastic, higher profits~~. Thus, even without direct communication, the rivals will be able to reach and maintain supracompetitive prices by the simple stratagem of observing each other's behavior in the marketplace and acting consistently with their group interest. Such action is fully consistent with the self-interest of each oligopolist. Each obviously benefits from taking account of rivals' reaction to its own behavior. Each recognizes that mutual interdependence means that coordinated behavior is rational, and trying to "go it alone" is suicidal.

ECONOMIST: That's precisely the point. In a market that is genuinely competitive, firms will indeed "go it alone." For example, in a market inhabited by 100 firms, each firm will be gung-ho to increase its profits by expanding sales and gaining market share. It will do so without taking account of the reaction of its rivals. It will feel too small and insignificant to have any effect on the market. Hence, it will act independently—without regard to the impact of its actions on its rivals or on the market as a whole. And since the other firms will reason the same way, and behave likewise, the end result will be genuine competition.

In short, where numbers are large, prices will be set by competition. Where numbers are small, prices will be set by overt or tacit collusion.

MODERATOR: I am afraid it will be impossible for us tonight to agree whether cigarette prices are determined by collusion or oligopolistic rationality. But are there other aspects of cigarette pricing that may be of interest to our viewers?

ECONOMIST: Yes, indeed: the recurrent resort to predatory tactics to prevent the entry of newcomers or to discipline rivals who refuse to play the oligopoly game.

MODERATOR: Please explain.

ECONOMIST: One example is the action of the major companies against the so-called ten-cent brands—an action roundly condemned by the Supreme Court.[6] We have already noted that in the depths of the Great Depression Reynolds led an industrywide price increase on the standard brands to 13¢ per pack. As economic theory would have predicted, this triggered a flood of entry by new competitors who appealed to price-conscious consumers.

The success of the "economy" or ten-cent brands was unprecedented. By June of 1932, they had captured 9 percent of the cigarette market; by November, their share reached 23 percent. The competitive impact on the Big Four, of course, was equally dramatic. The sales of their standard brands plunged nearly 30 percent within a two-year period.[7]

In order to contain this competition, the oligpolists launched a lethal cost-price

squeeze against the newcomers. They started
buying cheaper tobacco leaves (not used in
the manufacture of their own standard brands)
so as to raise the cost of such tobacco to a
point that the economy cigarettes made from
such tobacco could not be sold at a
sufficiently low price to compete with the
major brands of the oligopolists.[8]

At the same time, the dominant firms
slashed prices to such an extent that Camels
and Lucky Strikes were actually sold at a
loss. The combined net income of the
oligopolists during this interlude plunged an
average of 45 percent, with some of them
suffering individual profit declines as large
as 60 percent.[9]

The newcomers could not withstand this
predatory onslaught. Their market share
slipped from a high of 23 percent to 17
percent, then to 6 percent, and eventually to
insignificance. To them, predation proved
catastrophic. To the oligopolists, it was an
investment—although a costly one—that had
to be made to eliminate competition.

ATTORNEY: You call it predation. I call it good old-
fashioned competition. What would you
expect the established producers to have done
when the ten-cent brands first appeared?
Welcome them with open arms? Tell them
that it's OK to steal market share from the
established firms? Take a share of their
profits? Be a constant burr in their saddle?
That wouldn't be rational, would it? Even
economists would have to agree that, in our

free enterprise system, we can hardly expect firms to act in an irrational, suicidal fashion.

ECONOMIST: I am afraid you miss the point. Predation is a competitive practice that destroys the very essence of competition. We have seen how the old trust used it to monopolize the entire tobacco industry. We have seen how the oligopoly used it some 20 years later to protect its private hunting preserve from the challenge of newcomers. And we have seen, once again, in the late 1980s, how predatory sharpshooting contained the challenge of the producers of low-price generic cigarettes.

ATTORNEY: In that last instance you mention, you may recall that the Supreme Court did not buy into your predation theory.[10]

ECONOMIST: That's because the Court chose to embrace an abstract, abstruse, theoretical model concocted by otherworldly economic theorists rather than examine the indisputable facts of the case. Although it ruled against the "generics," the Court, nevertheless, conceded what is common knowledge—that "cigarette manufacturing has long been one of America's most concentrated industries"; that "for decades, production has been dominated by six firms" without significant challenge by new entry; that "the cigarette industry also has long been one of America's most profitable, in part because for many years there was no significant price competition among the rival firms"; that "list prices for cigarettes increased in lock-step, twice a year, for a number of years, irrespective of the rate of inflation, changes in the cost of production, or shifts in consumer demand."[11] That's hardly the profile of an effectively competitive industry—one that we can point to with pride as an exemplar of our free enterprise system.

MODERATOR: If it is indeed true that the cigarette industry is a cartel in which price competition is generally suppressed—whether by "oligopolistic rationality" or by tacit collusion—does this mean that there is no competition at all in the cigarette industry? What about the role of nonprice competition? What about competitive advertising? Competitive research and development? Competitive innovation?

ATTORNEY: I'm glad that you've finally gotten around to this aspect of the industry. There may not be much price competition, but the intensity of nonprice competition more than compensates for it. Take advertising, for example. The industry ranks among the heaviest advertisers in the country. In 1995, according to the Federal Trade Commission, it spent nearly $5 *billion* on cigarette advertising and promotion.[12] Philip Morris alone spent more than $1 billion, making it the third largest advertiser in the United States—only slightly behind General Motors and Proctor & Gamble. How are we to explain these massive expenditures? Obviously, the companies are engaged in a dog fight to gain market share at the expense of their competitors.

ECONOMIST: That's only one explanation. Another is that prodigious advertising expenditures erect a formidable barrier to entry. If not for this cost, many new firms would come into the industry and undermine the dominance of the incumbent oligopolists. This is not an industry in which there are any significant economies of scale in manufacturing.

ATTORNEY: Be that as it may, advertising is the principal technique of competition in this industry. It explains the constant shifts in the rise and fall of individual companies. It proves that the allegations of collusion and other cartel-like behavior that you and other critics like to level against the industry are without foundation.

ECONOMIST: A look at the record shows quite the contrary. It shows that what started as competitive advertising eventually led to collusion and concerted action.

MODERATOR: Do you have any facts to support that claim?

ECONOMIST: Let's look at the history of cigarette advertising. In 1953, *The Reader's Digest* published an article, "Cancer by the Carton," which bluntly stated that "used to excess, tobacco may shorten life." In 1952, the *British Medical Journal* published an article that reverberated around the world. It reported on a study of 1,465 lung cancer patients that showed a close correlation between heavy smoking and the disease.[13]

ATTORNEY: Statistical correlations are not the same as establishing cause. Such exercises sometimes lead to absurd conclusions. A couple of years ago, for example, the animal rights zealots claimed that "Michigan children are nearly three times as likely to be neglected and are twice as likely to be physically abused or sexually assaulted if they live in a county with either an above average or above median rate of hunting participation."[14] Obviously, some correlations are spurious.

ECONOMIST: Nevertheless, the "scare" stories in the popular press had a profound impact. After rising during the first half of the 20th century, per capita cigarette consumption began to decline in 1953 and 1954. The industry was concerned. According to one of its officials, "If every smoker in the country smoked one cigarette less a day, it would knock 5 percent off our sales."[15] Something had to be done.

MODERATOR: What, in fact, did the industry do?

ECONOMIST: It decided that it had to stop the oligopolists from making competing health claims about the relative health risks of each others' products. It had to stop the companies from screaming at the top of their lungs about nicotine, cigarette hangovers, smoker's cough, mildness, and kindred subjects. It had to deter companies from advertising that their cigarette "takes the fear out of smoking" or that their filter is "what the doctor ordered."

MODERATOR: How did they propose to accomplish that goal?

ECONOMIST: By agreement, collusion, and concerted action.

ATTORNEY: Nonsense! Big Tobacco has always been keenly aware of the antitrust laws and its prohibitions. As I remember it from my days in the industry, my own company had a strict "Antitrust Compliance Program" dating back to the early 1970s. It stated with unmistakable clarity: "It is the policy of the Company to conduct its operations in strict compliance with all applicable antitrust and trade regulation laws. The laws are based upon the principle of conserving and encouraging a free and competitive marketplace—a principle to which [the Company] wholeheartedly subscribes. The decisions made on behalf of this Company are to be without collusion, agreement, or understanding with competitors. The law requires a business to act alone in making competitive decisions."[16] Does this leave any doubt about the companies' stand on antitrust matters?

ECONOMIST: The statement of policy is perfectly clear. Unfortunately, the actions of Big Tobacco have not conformed to that policy. Remember the old saw? "It ain't what you pray for that counts; it's what you bet on."

ATTORNEY: Those are pretty serious charges. What proof do you have?

ECONOMIST: There is substantial direct evidence of a long-standing, explicit agreement among the companies not to compete on rival health claims in their advertising.

The first such agreement, dated in 1953, was contained in a planning memorandum under the subtitle "Things to Do." It says: "Develop some understanding with companies that, on *this* problem, none is going to seek competitive advantage by inferring to the public that *its* product is less risky than others. (No claims that special filters or toasting, or expert selection of tobacco, or extra length in the butt, or anything else, makes a given brand less likely to cause you-know-what. No 'Play-Safe-with-Luckies' idea—or with Camels or with anything else."[17] Such an understanding, the company presidents insisted, would be "a long-term, continuing program."[18]

And the agreement worked: Camel, which a year earlier had plumped the theme that "more doctors smoke Camels than any other cigarette," began sending the quite different message that "Camels agree with more people." Philip Morris, which had headlined "the cigarette that takes fear out of smoking," began writing lyrics about "vintage tobacco for pleasure." Pall Mall pulled back from the advice to "guard against throat scratch" and substituted "the pleasure of smoother smoking." Even filter-tip leader Viceroy changed its tune from "double-barreled protection" to "double your smoking pleasure."[19]

No more talk of health concerns—just comfortable, reassuring phrases about the good taste of cigarettes. Overnight, it seems, smoking a particular brand was no longer a health cure. It had become pure pleasure.

ATTORNEY: The decision to stop this "fear" advertising
              was made for one very good reason. It was a
              response to the Federal Trade Commission's
              cigarette advertising guidelines that were
              designed to curb exorbitant health claims.[20] It
              was an effort to cooperate with the
              government.

ECONOMIST: There is further evidence of the agreement to
              forgo damaging statements about rival
              companies. When the United States Tobacco
              Company circulated a "Dear Doctor" letter,
              which urged doctors to recommend its King
              Sano cigarette to "patients who enjoy
              smoking but who should reduce their intake
              of nicotine and tar," the president of Philip
              Morris thought this was a clear violation of
              the cartel agreement and wrote the following
              letter to the chairman of TIRC, the industry's
              joint research committee:

                        I am enclosing for your information a
                   letter which the United States Tobacco
                   Company is circulating to doctors. The
                   letter is self-explanatory in its contents,
                   and I am sure you will concur that it is
                   not consistent with what we have been
                   trying to accomplish in the industry in
                   the past four years.
                        Perhaps you can diplomatically
                   persuade Whitney Peterson [of U.S.
                   Tobacco Co.] that this kind of a letter
                   should not be circulated further or
                   repeated. . . .
                        It is one thing for *The Reader's
                   Digest* to make accusations about the
                   industry, but it is entirely another matter,

and perhaps a much more serious one, for a respected company in the industry to make [damaging] statements about competitive brands.[21]

ATTORNEY: That's stale evidence, going back to the 1950s.

ECONOMIST: On another occasion, in the 1970s, when an employee of U.S. Tobacco Company told a reporter that smokeless tobacco poses the least danger to health and that "it's only when you light tobacco that you start doing damage,"[22] the general counsel of U.S. Tobacco hastened to insist that the statement was unauthorized. Recognizing that the statement was in violation of cartel understandings, he promptly apologized to each of the cigarette companies and assured them that the employee in question was no longer employed at U.S. Tobacco.

ATTORNEY: That's some more anecdotal and episodic storytelling.

ECONOMIST: The pattern continued into the 1980s and beyond. In 1981, when Brown & Williamson [a subsidiary of British American Tobacco Co., or B.A.T.] introduced the Barclay brand, claiming that it was "99% tar free" and contained only 1mg of tar, Philip Morris and RJR complained to the Federal Trade Commission (FTC) that Barclay was engineered to give falsely low tar measurements by FTC standards. The commission, in turn, brought suit against

Brown & Williamson on grounds of deceptive advertising.[23]

ATTORNEY: Note that this action was taken, not by the industry, but by the Federal Trade Commission, an official agency of the U.S. government.

ECONOMIST: But that's not the end of the story. Philip Morris went across the Atlantic to attack the Barclay claims. In an ad that appeared in leading Dutch newspapers, it claimed that not Barclay but it, Philip Morris, was the "manufacturer of real low tar and nicotine cigarettes."

This triggered an outraged response from the chairman of B.A.T. In a telex to the president of Philip Morris in New York, he wrote: "I find it incomprehensible that Philip Morris would weigh so heavily the short-term commercial advantage from deprecating a competitor's brand. . . . In doing so, Philip Morris not only makes a mockery of *Industry cooperation* on smoking and health issues, but also appears to inaugurate a free-for-all in which illegal conduct is condoned provided the commercial stakes are high enough."[24]

ATTORNEY: The incident proves just how intense the advertising competition was and is among the major cigarette companies.

ECONOMIST: It also shows how such sporadic outbreaks of competition are resolved by collusion at the highest level of the tobacco industry. The matter was finally brought to a close in a telephone conversation between Hugh Cullman, the president of Philip Morris

International, and E. E. A. Bruell, the chairman of B.A.T. International. As we see in Graphic 3–5, Mr. Cullman clearly recognized that the Philip Morris ad was a breach of the industry's standing agreement. He readily conceded that it is "essential Industry hang together"; that "Holland activity was not company policy"; that "they must try to prevent this happening in the future." Mr. Bruell, in turn, stated that it is "essential to ensure that in the future no member of the Industry does anything similar."[25] That's not competition; it's collective action to suppress competition.

ATTORNEY: In any event, since the late 1960s, this whole advertising issue is really moot. At that time, with full approval of the government the cigarette makers jointly agreed to terminate all electronic media advertising.

ECONOMIST: That shouldn't be surprising. The industry was afraid that unless it did so, the Federal Communications Commission, under its "Fairness Doctrine," might make free advertising available to antitobacco interests.

ATTORNEY: You may call it collusion, but the industry also established—again with government approval—a Voluntary Cigarette Advertising Code to develop uniform standards for such advertising. It provided that no representations with respect to health shall be made unless the code's administrator ruled that they were based on "adequate, relevant, and valid scientific data." [26] Before you call this

Graphic 3-5

Telephone conversation between Hugh Cullman (H.C.), president of Philip Morris International (PM), and E. E. A. Bruell (E.B.), president of British American Tobacco Company (BAT), 26th October 1983.

H.C.	Essential Industry hang together. Holland activity was not PM company policy. They must try to prevent this happening in the future. Happy to say this to the INFOTAB Board and anything else EB would like stated.
E.B.	Concerned that this should never happen again and therefore PM's message should go out to all parts of the world. If (a) the statement is made by PM and (b) it is sent out by INFOTAB or PM, we would be much closer to a solution. Still need to check with PS.
H.C.	Understand there to be two issues: (a) All PM companies to be told. (b) Statement to be reinforced by other member companies of INFOTAB.
E.B.	Agree subject to Don Hoel (DH) legal approval.
H.C.	Currently looking at the legal angle. For clarity repeated—"PM to instruct its No. 1's they must not use anti-smoking activities, statements or programs for competitive gain." What happens if people broke the rule?
E.B.	Would expect PM to take drastic action with offender
H.C.	PS telex to CW yet received. . . .
E.B.	Could H.C. advise his overseas companies to inform BAT overseas companies about the message so they can feed back to E.B. Essential to ensure that in future no member of the Industry does anything similar.
H.C.	Did not know what disciplinary action was taken this time. Now sees the ramifications of the issue as a whole.

Source: State of Minnesota v. Philip Morris, Inc., Trial Exhibit No. 11,934.

collusion, let me remind you that the industry's code was cleared with the Antitrust Division of the Department of Justice.

ECONOMIST: All you are saying is that the government cooperated with the industry to make the cartel work more effectively. Incidentally, Lorillard later withdrew from the Advertising Code in order to be free to advertise its low tar and nicotine brands.[27]

MODERATOR: Let's move on to look at other elements of nonprice competition. What about innovation rivalry in the industry?

ECONOMIST: The Minnesota trial of the tobacco companies produced ample evidence of collusive arrangements to stifle research and innovation. In the postwar years, according to an RJR document, two "gentleman's agreements" were operative.[28] One specified that any company developing a technique for making a "safe" cigarette would share the discovery with others in the industry.

Therefore, when asked to fund a research proposal by Temple University scientists, an RJR executive wrote: "There is a *clear-cut agreement among all U.S. cigarette manufacturers* that any scientific discovery made within the companies, or otherwise sponsored by a single company, which might have a positive impact on the smoking and health controversy, would have to be freely shared, without any costs to the other manufacturers. There would, therefore, be no incentive for RJR to sponsor the [Temple] project. This applies to any other product development oriented research by a medical institution to be sponsored by a U.S. tobacco company."[29]

ATTORNEY: It would have been foolish for one company to fund such research. It would have duplicated the work of the TRC, the joint industry research institution, which was established in the early 1950s.

ECONOMIST: Concentrating research decisions in the TRC, which was run by industry attorneys rather than by scientists, meant of course that each company's incentive to compete was substantially abated, if not eliminated altogether.

ATTORNEY: I repeat that the rationale for industrywide research was to prevent duplication of effort and enhance efficiency.

ECONOMIST: The second "gentleman's agreement" provided that no individual company would do in-house biomedical research on intact animals.[30] Although the companies constantly spied on one another to ensure that all cartel members complied with the agreement, and although they occasionally tried to "cheat" on this agreement, they all adhered to the philosophy articulated by one of their members: "We won't start a war, but if war comes, we aim to fight well and win."

The extent to which the companies went to enforce their "gentleman's agreement" often bordered on the ludicrous. When Philip Morris president Cullman learned that RJR was in fact conducting in-house research on live animals, and after he had obtained the precise floor plans of the laboratory in which this research was going on, he protested this violation of the industry agreement to his RJR counterpart, President Galloway. The upshot was that RJR's so-called Mouse House was promptly shut down, 26 of its research personnel peremptorily dismissed, and the rest transferred to other activities in the company.[31] The shutdown, a BAT memo explained, was related to the industry's "tacit agreement between the heads of the U.S. companies" not to conduct "in-house biological research."[32]

ATTORNEY: It would have been a sheer waste for individual companies to conduct such research. It was much more efficient and economical for the industry to concentrate such research in the CTR—the Council for Tobacco Research. The industry felt that the CTR was its best chance for achieving major breakthroughs on the research front.

ECONOMIST: The CTR was a sham—a fig leaf to cover the industry's failure to address the problem of smoking and health. When the industry formed the CTR in 1954, it promised to research smoking and health issues. By 1993, only 10 of 296 CTR-funded projects had anything to do with tobacco and health.[33] "Let's face it," the director of the Philip Morris research department wrote to his CEO. "We are interested in evidence which we believe denies the allegation that cigarette smoking causes disease."[34]

Even the president of Lorillard was fed up with the domination of the CTR by a committee of industry lawyers. In 1978, in a candid moment, he wrote: "(1) We have again 'abdicated' the scientific research directional management of the Industry to the 'Lawyers' with virtually *no* involvement on the part of the scientific or business management side of the business. (2) Lorillard's management is opposed to the total Industry future being in the hands of the Committee of Counsel—it's reminiscent of the late 1960s when [the lawyers'] groups ran the TI [Tobacco Institute], CTR and everything else involved with the industry's public posture."[35]

ATTORNEY: How naïve can you be? This is a litigious society, and lawyers are everywhere. With all the government regulation and intrusion into the private sector, it's the rare CEO who dares to make decisions without first getting legal counsel. And that goes not only for corporations but for all organizations. With all the litigation against tobacco companies, how can anybody be surprised by the prominent role of lawyers in the industry!

MODERATOR: What about innovation? Didn't some of the companies try to introduce a "safer" cigarette?

ECONOMIST: There was certainly a tremendous incentive to do so. And the companies were aware of it.

In 1958, a Philip Morris document on long-range planning predicted that "the first company to produce a cigarette claiming a substantial reduction (say 50 percent less the present Parliament and Kent) in tars and nicotine, or an ersatz cigarette whose smoke contains no tobacco tars, and with good smoking flavor, will take the market."[36]

In 1966, the research director of Lorillard opined that the development of a cigarette, the smoke condensate from which gives little or no tumorigenic response, would "place the corporation in a highly enviable position, and in the writer's opinion a twofold or threefold increase in sales could result within a short period."[37]

In 1983, an RJR executive wrote: "The company which can produce [safer] products, which also supply a degree of user satisfaction which approaches that of current cigarette products, will become the dominant company in the industry almost overnight. It is reasonable to assume that the company who introduces such a product might capture as much as 25 share points in the first year if supply could keep pace with demand."[38]

ATTORNEY: It didn't take a genius to calculate the rewards for producing a "safer" cigarette. And the tobacco companies responded to the challenge.

In the 1950s, the industry started marketing filter cigarettes and followed up with the introduction of perforated filters in the 1970s. All the while, each of the companies continued its aggressive research efforts to come up with the ultimate prize—the "safer" cigarette.

In the 1960s, for example, British American Tobacco inaugurated Project Ariel —"a research topic aimed at the development of a smoking device from which a smoker can receive, in a suitable form, sufficient nicotine to give satisfactory physiological and psychological responses, unaccompanied by the products of combustion and pyrolysis associated with normal cigarette smoking."[39]

Similarly, some two years before the publication of the first surgeon general's report in 1964, Philip Morris "undertook to develop a physiologically superior product." The effort was successful. According to its internal evaluations, Philip Morris "did put together a charcoal filter product with performance superior to anything in the marketplace. That product was known as Saratoga. Physiologically, it was an outstanding cigarette."[40]

In the mid-1970s, Liggett developed its version of a "safer" cigarette—the so-called X-A. In laboratory tests on mice, the X-A proved to be "an effective means of treating 'tars' that reduce carcinomas [i.e., cancerous tumors] by 70 to 80 percent."[41]

In 1987, R. J. Reynolds unveiled its Premier cigarette, a new product that heated tobacco but did not burn it. According to the company's evaluations, "it was a smoking product with the benefits and advantages of current cigarettes but without many of the perceived negatives. The product . . . is the biggest technological breakthrough in the cigarette industry over the past thirty years."[42]

MODERATOR: What happened to these "safer" cigarettes? Contrary to predictions, none of them have swept the market. Why?

ATTORNEY: Consumers just didn't go for these new products. They didn't taste like a real cigarette. They didn't feel like a real cigarette.

ECONOMIST: As you well know, there were other reasons.

ATTORNEY: You can't blame the companies. They certainly tried to make the new products succeed. They test marketed them. They tried to persuade consumers of their virtues. But to no avail. So after a while, the products were withdrawn from the market.

ECONOMIST: A number of factors may have contributed to the demise of these innovative products, but the paramount reason was the unwillingness of the manufacturers to tell the whole story. Bound by the cartel's agreement not to make any health claims in their advertising, nor to make any admissions about conventional cigarettes as a cause of disease, nor to make any claim of product superiority in comparison to existing brands, the companies were restricted to using pusillanimous and ineffective advertising slogans to tout the new products. No wonder they failed.

   According to R. J. Reynolds, "Premier failed for reasons that are well understood. The concept addressed the greatest latent demand in the industry. It was not executed and presented to the consumer in an effective way. The . . . product advantages were prevented from being communicated effectively."[43] Instead, Premier was touted as "a cleaner smoke," with little or no side-stream emissions.

Philip Morris's Saratoga failed for much the same reasons. According to the company's research director, the public was kept ignorant of "its physiological superiority."[44]

Liggett's X-A failed in part because the company was reluctant to advertise its health benefits. The company's president "was told by someone in the Philip Morris Company that if [Liggett] tried to market such a product that they would clobber us."[45]

In short, the consumer was never squarely presented with the trade-off between safety and health, on the one hand, and "better taste," on the other. Had the companies been candid about this trade-off in their marketing and advertising, their "safer" cigarettes would have enjoyed a far greater commercial success.[46]

ATTORNEY: If you are right, how do you explain the hundreds of millions of dollars, perhaps billions of dollars, that the companies laid on the line to support the new products?

ECONOMIST: I think it amounted to something like $3 billion —over a period of four decades. But that is a trifling amount compared to the resources at their command and the total of roughly $47 billion they spent on advertising and promotion.

A look at Graphic 3-6 is revealing. It reflects where the companies put their priorities. They spent an average of 13 percent of their sales revenue on advertising and promotion, but less than a miniscule 1 percent on research and development, and one-hundredth of 1 percent on programs to prevent youth smoking.

Graphic 3-7 tells the same story in dollar amounts. That about sums up what the U.S. tobacco industry is all about.

MODERATOR: I am afraid we are running out of time. I must ask that each of you conclude with a 30-second summary of your position.

ATTORNEY: In an industry like cigarettes, it is idle to expect dog-eat-dog price competition. Such rivalry would be suicidal. However, the cigarette companies do engage in vigorous nonprice rivalry. Advertising competition, although it is kept within the government's rules against false and misleading health claims, is vigorous and intense. Above all, the individual companies are in a fierce and continual battle to find and develop a "safe" cigarette compatible with public health and welfare.

ECONOMIST: The cigarette industry is a tight-knit cartel that systematically eschews both price and nonprice competition. Its members are tied to one another in a mosaic of anticompetitive arrangements and collusive actions. It is not by accident, but in accordance with common agreements, that they follow policies of

112 The Tobacco Wars

Graphic 3-6

TOBACCO COMPANY SALES; RESEARCH AND DEVELOPMENT EXPENDITURES; ADVERTISING, MARKETING, AND PROMOTION EXPENDITURES; AND YOUTH PREVENTION EXPENDITURES
(percentage)

	Philip Morris	R. J. Reynolds	B & W	American	Lorillard	Liggett
Advertising, Marketing, and Promotion Expenditures to Total Domestic Tobacco Sales	13.60	16.20	15.20	8.70	14.60	10.70
Research and Development Expenditures to Total Domestic Tobacco Sales	.90	1.20	.30	.30	.60	.50
Youth Prevention Expenditures to Total Domestic Tobacco Sales	.020	.032	.002	.005	.006	.004
Research and Development Expenditures to Advertising, Marketing and Promotion Expenditures	6.70	6.60	1.90	3.80	4.30	4.40
Youth Prevention Expenditures to Advertising, Marketing and Promotion Expenditures	.10	.10	.013	.034	.041	.025

Source: Minnesota Tobacco Litigation (1998); calculated from testimony of Paul J. Much, March 23, 1998.

Graphic 3-7

TOBACCO COMPANY SALES; RESEARCH AND DEVELOPMENT EXPENDITURES;
ADVERTISING, MARKETING, AND PROMOTION EXPENDITURES;
AND YOUTH PREVENTION EXPENDITURES (1954–94)

(thousands of dollars)

	Philip Morris	R.J. Reynolds	B & W	American	Lorillard	Liggett
Total Sales	$141,442,700	$118,621,737	$50,209,589	$50,769,596	$36,100,506	$19,999,120
R & D Expenditures	1,258,415	1,233,199	142,065	168,033	204,901	94,366
Advertising, Marketing, and Promotion	18,390,313	9,733,297	7,616,377*	4,439,542	4,733,843	2,130,330
Youth Prevention Expenditures	20,819	19,100	643	918	1,336	N/A

*Does not include data, 1954–57.

Source: Minnesota Tobacco Litigation (1998); calculated from testimony of Paul J. Much, March 23, 1998.

conscious parallel action. As we say in Texas,
"When you see a turtle on top of a fence post,
you know it didn't get there by accident."

MODERATOR: Thank you both for your frank and articulate
statements. Our time has run out for tonight.
Please join us again next week, when we shall
discuss the social welfare aspects of the
tobacco industry. Good night!

REFERENCES

[1] Quoted in Richard Hofstadter, *Social Darwinism in American Thought,* (Boston: Beacon Press, 1955), p. 45.

[2] United States v. American Tobacco Co., 221 U.S. 106 (1911).

[3] New York Times, April 27, 1994, p. C6.

[4] William B. Burnett, "Predation by a Nondominant Firm: The Liggett Case," in *The Antitrust Revolution,* ed. John E. Kwoka and Lawrence J. White (New York: HarperCollins Publishers, 1994), p. 281.

[5] Stephen J. Adler and Alix M. Freedman, "Tobacco Suit Exposes Ways Cigarette Firms Keep the Profits Fat," *The Wall Street Journal,* March 5, 1990, p. A5.

[6] American Tobacco Co. v. United States, 328 U.S. 781 (1946).

[7] American Tobacco Co., v. United States, 328 U.S. 781, 806 (1946); William H. Nicholls, *Price Policies in the Cigarette Industry* (Nashville, TN: Vanderbilt University Press, 1951), p. 112.

[8] American Tobacco Co. v. United States, 328 U.S. 781, pp. 803–804.

[9] Nicholls, *Price Policies in the Cigarette Industry,* pp. 91, 105, 120.

[10] Brooke Group v. Brown & Williamson Tobacco Co., 113 S. Ct. 2578 (1993).

[11] Id. at 2582, 2583.

[12] FTC, *Report to the Congress for 1995, Pursuant to the Federal Cigarette Labeling and Advertising Act.*

[13] See *Business Week,* Dec. 5, 1952, Jan. 2, 1954, and June 19, 1954.

[14] "Michigan Stats Confirm Hunting, Child Abuse Link," *Animal People,* (October 1995).

[15] *Business Week,* Dec. 5, 1953, p. 64.

[16] State of Minnesota v. Philip Morris, Inc., Trial Exhibit No. 13,763 (1998).

[17] State of Minnesota v. Philip Morris, Inc., Trial Exhibit No. 18,904 (1998); emphases in the original.

[18] State of Minnesota v. Philip Morris, Inc., Trial Exhibit No. 18,905 (1998).

[19] *Business Week,* June 19, 1954, p. 58.

[20] John E. Calfee, "The Ghosts of Cigarette Advertising Past," *Regulation* (Summer 1997), pp. 38–45.

[21] Letter from Joseph F. Cullman III to Timothy V. Hartnett, July 8, 1957.

[22] *New York Post,* March 16, 1977.

[23] FTC v. Brown & Williamson, 778 F.2d 35, 38 (D.C. Cir. 1985).

[24] State of Minnesota v. Philip Morris, Inc., Trial Exhibit No. 10,933 (1998); emphasis supplied.

[25] State of Minnesota v. Philip Morris, Inc., Trial Exhibit No. 11,934 (1998).

[26] "Tobacco Industry Voluntary Cigarette Advertising Code," issued Jan 1., 1965.

[27] Dow Jones News Service, March 28, 1966.

[28] State of Minnesota v. Philip Morris, Inc., Trial Exhibit No. 3305 (1998).

[29] Memorandum by Frank G. Colby to Dr. Roy E. Morse, Oct. 26, 1981 (emphasis supplied).

[30] State of Minnesota v. Philip Morris, Inc., Trial Exhibits No. 2544 and 2549 (1998).

[31] State of Minnesota v. Philip Morris, Inc., Trial Exhibit No. 12,756 (1998).

[32] Cited in Order of the District Court, Second Judicial District, State of Minnesota, in State of Minnesota v. Philip Morris, Inc., Jan. 26, 1998.

[33] State of Minnesota v. Philip Morris, Inc., Trial Exhibit No. 4700 (1998).

[34] Letter from Wakeham to Cullman, cited in State of Minnesota v. Philip Morris, Inc., Trial Transcript, Mar. 20, 1998.

[35] State of Minnesota v. Philip Morris, Inc., Trial Exhibit No. 10,165 (1998).

[36] State of Minnesota v. Philip Morris, Inc., Trial Exhibit No. 11,662 (1998).

[37] State of Minnesota v. Philip Morris, Inc., Trial Exhibit No. 14,020 (1998).

[38] State of Minnesota v. Philip Morris, Inc., Trial Exhibit No. 12,509 (1998).

[39] State of Minnesota v. Philip Morris, Inc., Trial Exhibit No. 11,942 (1998).

[40] State of Minnesota v. Philip Morris, Inc., Trial Exhibit No. 11,663 (1998).

[41] State of Minnesota v. Philip Morris, Inc., Trial Exhibit No. 11,523 (1998).

[42] State of Minnesota v. Philip Morris, Inc., Trial Exhibit No. 12,873 (1998).

[43] State of Minnesota v. Philip Morris, Inc., Trial Exhibit No. 13,082 (1998).

[44] State of Minnesota v. Philip Morris, Inc., Trial Exhibit No. 11,663 (1998).

[45] Deposition of Dr. James Mold, Liggett Researcher, in Cipollone v. Liggett, Jan. 11, 1988.

[46] See e.g., State of Minnesota v. Philip Morris, Inc., Trial Exhibit No. 11,632 (1998).

IV. The Social Welfare Front

MODERATOR: Welcome to the fourth program in our series, *The Tobacco Wars*. Tonight we address the social welfare implications of the market for tobacco products: Does the business of consuming and producing tobacco harm society? If so, in what ways? With what results? And how, if at all, can the magnitude of this damage to social welfare be measured?

Economists teach that the free marketplace behaves according to the laws of supply and demand. These laws, they say, govern the economic decisions made by individual buyers and sellers, and transform them into a mechanism for promoting the public good. In Adam Smith's famous phrase, the free market operates as if by an "invisible hand" to optimally allocate society's resources in accordance with consumer preferences, and to promote the well-being of all.

But is tobacco fundamentally different? Does individual behavior in this case violate the laws of supply and demand? Does it pit private interest against social welfare? Does the "magic of the marketplace" fail to operate? And if so, does this breakdown require extensive government regulation and control in order to protect the common good?

To explore these questions, we're joined tonight by two panelists: a physician from the organization Stop Tobacco or Perish (STOP) and a spokeswoman from People United for Freedom (PUFF).

Welcome to both of you. Doctor, let's begin with you. In advocating tighter government regulation of smoking, you obviously believe a free market for tobacco is incapable of producing socially desirable results. Why is that?

STOP: Because smoking makes everyone in society worse off: It kills smokers, who harm themselves. It also harms the rest of us in at least two important ways: Physiologically, nonsmokers' suffer because we're forced to inhale the secondhand smoke emitted by smokers and, thus, we're forcibly exposed to the same sicknesses and diseases. Financially, we're worse off because we must all pay the medical costs of treating tobacco-caused diseases among smokers and nonsmokers alike.

In economic terms, smoking creates "negative externalities" and "social costs," which preclude the free marketplace from achieving socially optimal results.

MODERATOR: Why is that?

STOP: Because smokers make their decision without taking account of the harmful physiological and financial effects on themselves and others. They fail to take into account the full costs to society of their behavior.

MODERATOR: Are you suggesting that a free market for tobacco is tantamount to a free market for murder and suicide?

STOP: It may sound exaggerated but, yes, that's essentially correct. We don't tolerate murder—indeed, we prosecute people for committing it. I see no reason why tobacco should be treated any differently, given its lethal consequences.

PUFF: Nonsense!

MODERATOR: I take it you disagree.

PUFF: Absolutely.

MODERATOR: On what grounds?

PUFF: On the grounds that automobiles kill tens of thousands of people every year, but that doesn't imply the auto industry should be abolished. Airline crashes kill people. Should we eliminate air travel? Skiing, mountain climbing, swimming—all these activities are life-threatening. Does that mean we should prosecute skiers, mountain climbers, and swimmers and lock them away?

STOP: As a matter of fact, we *do* have laws regulating the activities you've just enumerated: automobile drivers must be licensed by the state. There is an intricate set of rules of the road—with citations and jail sentences imposed for violations. Airline pilots must be licensed, qualified, and certified. Lifeguards patrol swimming sites, and so forth.

PUFF: Those regulations obviously don't prevent people from drowning or dying in car accidents.

STOP: But they do limit the damage and death that would occur if these activities were unregulated.

PUFF: You can't prevent people from freely choosing to do something, so long as they're aware of the potential risks involved.

STOP: But smoking is addictive, so let's not pretend that any kind of "free choice" is involved.

MODERATOR: Please explain, Doctor, why you think addiction is incompatible with free choice.

STOP: Consider the following facts. Two-thirds of smoking adults wish they could quit. Seventeen million smokers try to stop smoking every year, but fewer than one out of ten actually succeeds. By some estimates, as many as 90 percent of all smokers admit they're addicted; eight out of ten say they wish they had never started smoking.[1]

PUFF: Half the people who live in Los Angeles say they want to leave![2] Are we to brand them as clinically deranged? People make many decisions that are not easily changed, including marriage, career, home purchase, regional location.[3] Does that imply that they should be prohibited from marrying, choosing their own career, or buying a home? Obviously not.

STOP: The difference is that once people start smoking, the addiction they acquire prevents them from exercising the "freedom of choice" to quit. They're incapable of controlling themselves. Their so-called freedom of choice must be constrained somehow, in order to stop them from hurting themselves and others.

MODERATOR: Doctor, is there a particular definition of "addiction" you're applying here?

STOP: The commissioner of the Food and Drug Administration recently delineated four attributes that together define a condition of addiction: first, compulsive use of something despite the knowledge that it's harmful; second, a "psychoactive" or direct chemical effect produced in the brain; third, reinforcing behavior that promotes additional use; and fourth, withdrawal symptoms when deprived of the substance. These are the hallmarks of an addictive substance. Nicotine and tobacco satisfy all four of them.[4]

PUFF: That's a gross distortion of the term *addiction* in order to justify an ideologically motivated crusade.

MODERATOR: In what way?

PUFF: Let me ask our viewers this question: As an airline passenger, would you have some qualms about boarding a plane piloted by someone who had just downed ten martinis, smoked crack cocaine, shot heroin, or popped a fistful of mind-altering pills? Of course you would. But would you have the same reaction if informed that the pilot had smoked a cigarette before the flight?[5] Would you recoil in horror or fear for your life? I don't think anybody would seriously consider cigarette smoking to be in the same league with cocaine and heroin addiction. Not even the good doctor!

MODERATOR: "Psychoactive" sounds like a definitive medical characteristic.

PUFF: Of course it does. That's why antismoking zealots trumpet it: it frightens people. But you must understand that many things affect the brain's chemistry and, thus, could be branded as psychoactive. These include food, water, sex, heat, cold, and colors. Sugar "causes" the consumer of a soft drink to continue drinking. Salad dressing "causes" humans to consume lettuce. Orgasms "cause" humans to continue sexual behavior.[6] Viewed in this light, tobacco consumption is no more "addictive" than coffee, tea or Twinkies.[7]

STOP: Addiction is not determined by any single physiological or behavioral characteristic. Once upon a time, addiction was clinically defined in terms of "criminality," "character deficit," and "immorality." But as Surgeon General Koop has explained, those conceptions are now recognized as irrelevant.

The sine qua non of addiction to a substance is that it governs behavior to such an extent that it is detrimental to the person or society *and* the individual is incapable of controlling his or her consumption of it.[8]

MODERATOR: I take it that addiction means something quite different for your organization?

PUFF: It certainly does. ~~We subscribe to the definition articulated by Surgeon General Terry in his 1964~~ report on smoking. ~~That report drew a sharp distinction between "habituation" and "addiction"~~ because—and I quote—"the biological effects of tobacco, like coffee and other caffeine-containing beverages, betel morsel chewing and the like, are not comparable to those produced by morphine, alcohol, barbiturates, and many other potent addicting drugs."[9] The 1964 report emphasized a key characteristic of addiction as—and I quote again—"a state of periodic or chronic intoxication."[10]

Chronic intoxication obviously doesn't apply to smokers, who think clearly, make difficult decisions without any interference from their smoking, and perform at high levels in their personal and professional lives.[11] True addictions, like heroin and cocaine, prevent users from performing normal functions like working, driving, and maintaining health family relationships. Tobacco consumption does not. Imagine how foolish it would be to arrest people for driving under the influence of cigarettes![12]

STOP: I think it's clear who's playing games with definitional semantics here. But don't take it from me. Consider how people in the tobacco industry view cigarettes and the addictive properties of nicotine. A high-ranking R. J. Reynolds official, in a confidential 1972 planning memorandum, candidly stated: "Tobacco products, uniquely, contain and deliver nicotine, a potent drug with a variety of physiological effects." He declared that "a tobacco product is, in essence, a vehicle for delivery of nicotine." He pointed out that the tobacco industry is "based upon design, manufacture and sale of attractive dosage forms of nicotine. . . . Happily for the tobacco industry," he emphasized, "nicotine is both habituating and unique in its variety of physiological actions, hence no other active material or combination of materials provides equivalent 'satisfaction'." And he warned if the industry were to reduce nicotine at the insistence of its critics, then it would "eventually liquidate our business."[13]

Now, what's he saying? He's saying that smokers are addicted to nicotine and, once hooked, can't shake the habit.

And, in fact, the tobacco companies have taken out numerous patents for controlling the amount of nicotine in cigarettes, increasing the amount of nicotine in cigarettes, manipulating the rate at which nicotine is delivered in cigarettes, and transferring nicotine from one material to another.[14]

I think they know addiction when they see it.

PUFF: Soft drink producers deliberately alter the amounts of caffeine they blend into their beverages! Do we describe their practices in sinister terms? Of course not! It's the magic of the marketplace catering to consumer preferences. Smokers, like consumers of other products, desire variety and choice, which the industry works to supply and improve upon.[15]

Labeling smoking as "addiction" is just a puritanical way of vilifying something that other people do that you don't like.

And by corrupting language in their effort to concoct non-existent maladies, antismokers defeat what they claim as their most important goal.

MODERATOR: How is that?

PUFF: They victimize smokers into believing they can't quit smoking even if they want to, so they won't even try. It also sends a terrible message to young people. Telling them that heroin and cocaine are no different than cigarette smoking effectively encourages the young to experiment with these truly dangerous, truly addictive, truly destructive hard drugs. It makes young people think that if millions of everyday, upright adults smoke tobacco, then cocaine and heroin use can't be too bad.[16]

The fact is that some 40 million Americans have stopped smoking. Indeed, the number of former smokers who have quit now exceeds the number of people who continue to smoke.[17]

STOP: Remember what Mark Twain said. Stopping smoking was the easiest thing he ever did, and he ought to know because he had done it hundreds of times.

PUFF: The president of every major tobacco company has sworn—under oath—that smoking is not addictive.[18]

STOP: That was in 1994. In 1998, however, the current chief executive officer of Philip Morris conceded before a congressional committee that smoking may be addictive under some definitions.[19]

PUFF: If you read his testimony carefully, you'll find that Mr. Bible, the CEO of Philip Morris, clearly refused to embrace those definitions on the grounds that they fail to meet the intoxication criterion.[20]

MODERATOR: What about the problem of nonsmokers? As the doctor indicated at the outset, they don't *choose* to smoke. Yet he says they're forced to inhale the smoke of others and to contract the smoking-induced diseases caused by others. He claims the rest of us don't choose to smoke, yet we must pay the medical costs of treating the smoking-related diseases that smokers inflict on themselves and everyone else.

PUFF: People whose houses don't burn down are "forced" through their insurance premiums to pay those whose homes do burn down. People who aren't involved in auto accidents are "forced" through their car insurance premiums to pay the expenses of those who are. By definition, insurance of all kinds,

including medical insurance, involves a
pooling of risk: I promise to pay your bills if
you get sick, and you promise to pay my bills
if I get sick. Insurance participants, in effect,
are one person. It's a reciprocal relationship
in which there is no "external" cost.[21]

MODERATOR: But people don't voluntarily choose to have
their homes destroyed in fires or to
voluntarily be involved in automobile
accidents.

STOP: If they do, they're prosecuted for arson and
homicide!

PUFF: We all are occasionally exposed to something
—or someone—we find objectionable. That's
simply the price of living among others in a
society.

STOP: We're not talking about a trivial nuisance
here. According to the Centers for Disease
Control, nearly 90 percent of nonsmoking
Americans are exposed to secondhand smoke,
based on an analysis of blood samples.[22]

PUFF: Tobacco isn't the only source of nicotine. It
occurs naturally in a variety of common
vegetables, including tomatoes, potatoes,
eggplants, and green peppers—all of which
are rather widely consumed.[23]

STOP: The difference, of course, is that people don't
die from consuming eggplant. They do die,
however, from inhaling tobacco smoke.

MODERATOR: Doctor, are there some estimates of the health threat posed by secondhand smoke?

STOP: It's enormous. According to the American Medical Association, "passive" smoking, or environmental tobacco smoke, may kill as many as 50,000 Americans annually, with 35,000 of these deaths due to heart disease, 3,000 from lung cancer, and about 12,000 from other cancers. Put differently, exposure to secondhand smoke is the third leading cause of premature death in the United States, exceeded only by direct smoking and alcohol.[24]

It's enormous. According to the American Medical Association, "passive" smoking, or environmental tobacco smoke, may kill as many as 50,000 Americans annually, with 35,000 of these deaths due to heart disease, 3,000 from lung cancer, and about 12,000 from other cancers. Put differently, exposure to secondhand smoke is the third leading cause of premature death in the United States, exceeded only by direct smoking and alcohol.[24]

The harm to innocent children is particularly tragic. Over 40 percent of children age five and younger live in a household with at least one smoker and are forced to breathe secondhand smoke. According to Congressman Henry Waxman, this exposure triggers or worsens asthma attacks in upwards of one million children annually; causes 150,000 to 300,000 cases of bronchitis, pneumonia, and other lower-respiratory-tract infections in children; and aggravates ear infections among infants.[25]

No wonder the Environmental Protection Agency (EPA) has classified secondhand tobacco smoke as a Class-A human carcinogen.

PUFF: The EPA estimates you just cited have been totally discredited! Let's look at the "junk science" used by the EPA to generate them.

In their attempt to fabricate a relationship between secondhand smoke and cancer, antismoking zealots at the EPA performed a "meta-analysis" on a pooled set of 30 inconsistent, separate statistical studies independently conducted by others. Six of those studies found that inhaling secondhand smoke actually *reduces* the risk of cancer among nonsmokers! One of them found the relative risk of heart disease to be higher for passive smokers than for active smokers! Twenty-four of those 30 studies found no statistically significant relationship in either direction.

In addition, the EPA's meta-analysis excluded studies that would have further undercut the disease and secondhand smoke connection but added studies that seemed to bolster it. The significance levels of the EPA's overall assessment were also manipulated until the desired statistical results was obtained.[26] Then—presto!—immense publicity is orchestrated by Congressman Waxman for unveiling a "scientific" study purporting to document his neurotic belief that the merest whiff of tobacco smoke sends millions to their deathbeds!

STOP: Congressman Waxman and the EPA have thoroughly rebutted those claims. Twenty-four of the 30 studies included in the EPA's analysis found a positive correlation between secondhand smoke and the incidence of lung cancer; 9 of them were, in fact, statistically significant. The excluded study was omitted because it was published after the EPA's study had been completed; moreover, the authors of the omitted study concluded that regulations restricting smoking in public places are "well founded."[27] I think the dangers of secondhand smoke have been amply documented.

PUFF: An in-depth study by the Congressional Research Service disagrees with you. After reviewing EPA and other studies, it finds the probability of death from lung cancer due to secondhand smoke to be two-tenths of 1 percent in the case of people whose spouses smoke, and only seven-hundredths of 1 percent for households in which neither spouse smokes.[28] For the entire nonsmoking population, the probability of death from passive smoking is estimated at .0043%—a level that puts secondhand smoke on a par with premature death from home accidents, homicide, drowning and fire.[29]

Similarly, the World Health Organization's recent seven-country European study failed to find any statistically significant link between secondhand smoke and disease.[30]

No wonder a U.S. district court threw out the EPA's second-hand smoking study as a perversion of both science and administrative procedure.[31]

MODERATOR: What about innocent children exposed to secondhand smoke?

PUFF: The evidence is highly mixed and contradictory. Of the ten studies of child asthma analyzed by the EPA, two reported no effect; another found no significant effect for girls and an effect for boys only if both parents smoked. One study dealt with responses to subfreezing air rather than asthma; one found no effect in the case of better-educated mothers; one found no effect when fewer than ten cigarettes were smoked in the home per day.[32] The designs of these studies differ so much, as do their results, that I don't see how any clear, convincing conclusion can be scientifically drawn from them.

Another highly curious aspect of that EPA study suggests that ideology—not science—is driving its findings.

MODERATOR: What's that?

PUFF: The EPA has performed meta-analyses examining the carcinogeneity of other substances besides tobacco smoke, including diesel exhaust fumes and electromagnetic radiation. Sixty percent of the constituent studies examined in the case of electromagnetic radiation indicated a statistically significant relationship between exposure and lung cancer incidence, while the corresponding rate for secondhand smoke was only 20 percent. Yet the EPA considered the evidence in the case of electromagnetic radiation—three times more powerful than secondhand smoke—to be too weak to justify regulatory action. Why does the EPA consider weaker results sufficient to justify radical action against tobacco, but far stronger results too weak to justify action against diesel fumes and electromagnetic radiation?[33] It is very suspicious to me.

So, too, is the fact that the World Health Organization quashed its recent findings that showed no statistical link between secondhand smoke and disease.[34]

STOP: Let's not fixate on just two isolated bits of evidence. ~~Mountains of other studies have been conducted—in the United States and elsewhere—finding connections between exposure to secondhand smoke and adverse health consequences.~~ These are surveyed and analyzed in the surgeon general's 1986 report,[35] a National Research Council study,[36] and a report by the International Agency for Research on Cancer.[37] There's no serious question concerning the link between tobacco smoke inhalation and the health threats it poses.

PUFF: But how *strong* are the links? That's the crucial question!

STOP: Strong enough to make secondhand smoke the third leading killer in the United States— more than all people killed in car accidents, more than twice the number of people murdered in homicides, more than twice as many people as die from AIDS.[38] If smoking kills smokers—and it does—it's obvious that it can kill nonsmokers too.

PUFF: Juries have consistently rejected that claim, including, most recently, the jury in a secondhand smoke trial in Indiana.[39]

Besides, "dose makes the poison" is a central maxim of toxicology. The smoke directly inhaled by smokers contains chemicals in concentrations up to a million times greater than that found in secondhand smoke.[40] Let me ask you: Do you consider chlorine to be carcinogenic?

STOP: In sufficient doses, anything is capable of inflicting death, even water.

PUFF: Well, I won't inquire into your bathing habits. The fact is that lots of studies have found *no* statistically significant relationship between exposure to secondhand smoke and the incidence of smoking-related diseases. As summarized in one survey, "There is no substantial evidence to support the view that exposure to environmental tobacco smoke presents a significant health hazard to nonsmokers."[41] A cooked hamburger contains more carcinogens than eight hours of breathing secondhand smoke![42]

STOP: If you really believe that, then why do so many people suffer allergic reactions when forced to breathe the smoke of others?

PUFF: Overcrowded and congested living conditions make people hypersensitive to the behavior of others.
        Because cigarette smoke is highly visible, smokers have become lightning rods for pent-up frustrations, anxieties, and general discontent.[43] Constantly bombarding people with exaggerated and scientifically unsubstantiated claims about the death threat

of smoking only feeds their frustrations with modern life. It only inflames their propensity to vilify smokers as the root of all evil.

MODERATOR:　Are you suggesting that the smoking-related symptoms suffered by nonsmokers are just figments of their imagination?

PUFF:　Actually, you raise a very interesting point. Allow me to recount a famous scientific story. For many years in a province of Alberta, Canada, complaints had been voiced about sour gas fumes emanating from a nearby mine. All kinds of diseases were imagined to be caused by inhaling those fumes—birth defects, cancers, and a host of other illnesses in that particular district. Finally, the Canadian government sponsored a large-scale scientific study to get to the bottom of the problem. In what has since been praised as one of the best epidemiological studies ever conducted, the scientific findings were remarkable: *No* excess birth defects! *No* excess cancers! *No* excess diseases of any kind could be identified!

What the scientists did find, however, was an excess of unfounded, imaginary symptoms reported by people in the community where the sour gas had been publicized as a problem. Yet in a nearby community—where the same fumes existed but had not been publicized—people reported no adverse symptoms.[44]

MODERATOR:　And your point is?

PUFF: ~~My point is that bombastic media hype~~
~~provides fertile grounds for cultivating~~
~~psychological fantasies about secondhand~~
~~smoke diseases—diseases that objective~~
~~scientists cannot document with any degree of~~
~~regularity, consistency, or confidence.~~

STOP: Do you deny that cigarette smoke is a form of
air pollution that nonsmokers find offensive?
Why should the rest of us be forced to choose
between enjoying a meal out and inhaling
toxic tobacco fumes versus staying home in
order to protect our health?[45]

PUFF: That argument is both specious and absurd.
Think of it rationally and dispassionately. Put
it in perspective. The state of California now
prohibits smoking in all restaurants—even
bars—ostensibly to protect its citizens from
air pollution. Yet when restaurant patrons step
out into the streets of Los Angeles, what do
they find? In a city that 60 years ago was
endowed with lush palm trees, fragrant
orange groves, and ocean-clean air, they now
find an ecological wasteland created by
millions of automobiles and thousands of
foul-smelling buses. The palm trees are dying
of petrochemical smog; the orange groves are
paved over by freeways; the air is a septic
tank into which millions of cars pump
thousands of tons of pollutants daily.

   These are cold facts, but what does the
state of California do about it? Does it launch
an Albigensian crusade against automobiles
as it does against cigarettes?

MODERATOR: Is the United States unique in its concern about the pollution caused by smoking?

PUFF: "Pollution" is a concept of cultural relativity. A dog licking its master's face doubtless would be considered "pollution" by some. Goats roaming in the house are not considered "pollution" in a great many parts of the world. Without culture, there is no meaningful conception of pollution.

Smoking has become a symbol and target for the broader forms of pollution— technology, media, politics—that offend people but which they feel powerless to fix.[46]

MODERATOR: So far, we've discussed the social costs of smoking in terms of health and disease. What about the financial costs? What do the health effects add up to in dollars and cents?

STOP: They, too, are immense. At the lower end, the Centers for Disease Control estimate the direct medical costs of smoking-related diseases to be in the order of $50 billion annually. Of this amount, 54 percent represents hospital expenditures; 31 percent represents physician expenses; 10 percent represents nursing home charges; 4 percent represents prescription drug charges; and 2 percent represents home health care costs.[47]

The Office of Technology Assessment puts the social costs higher, at approximately $70 billion per year. This total amount includes $21 billion in direct health care costs, and $47 billion in the lost future earnings resulting from death and debilitating illnesses.[48]

Other studies put the social cost even higher. The Treasury Department estimates them to be in excess of $100 billion per year,[49] while an EPA analysis implies the costs may be as great as $500 billion annually, depending on the dollar value assigned to human life.[50]

By any measure, tobacco inflicts a huge cost on American society! Smokers choose to smoke. The rest of us pay the price. And the tobacco companies reap the profit. That's the failure of a free market for tobacco. That's why government regulation is absolutely essential. That's why states are suing tobacco companies to recover health expenses borne on the backs of taxpayers!

PUFF: Wait a minute! What about the government revenues generated by tobacco sales? What about the cigarette excise taxes paid by smokers? Include those and other relevant factors and you'll find that, if anything, smokers are a net benefit to society.

MODERATOR: Now there's a claim that requires further explanation! How can smokers possibly benefit the rest of us?

PUFF: First, excise taxes on tobacco alone generate $13.5 billion in government revenues annually. Those tax payments go a considerable way toward compensating for the medical costs of treating smoking-related diseases.[51]

MODERATOR: What other considerations enter?

PUFF: If we accept the antismokers' arguments that tobacco kills, then smokers die at younger ages, correct?

MODERATOR: I'm with you.

PUFF: If smokers die younger, then they don't live to be as old as others, correct?

MODERATOR: At last, a proposition that is eminently noncontroversial!

PUFF: But if smokers don't live as long, then they require less of all the astronomically expensive health care required to treat the elderly. So they save society all those expenses too.

At the same time, smokers contribute funds to pension programs and Social Security in their younger years that they don't live long enough to recoup in old age—another benefit to nonsmokers who live longer and have more pension funds to draw on. The Office of Technology Assessment report you just cited points out that a significant reduction in smoking, and the attendant increase in life expectancy, would trigger increases in medical spending, Medicare outlays, and expenditures by Social Security and other government agencies.[52]

Take all those savings into account and smokers *save* society 32¢ per cigarette pack sold—a figure that rises to 85¢ per pack if we include excise tax revenues.[53] Smokers benefit us all—including nonsmokers![54]

STOP: What about the lost economic production that results from people dying at the most productive point in their career? On average, people who die from a smoking-related disease lose 12 to 15 years of life because of their tobacco consumption.[55] According to the Treasury Department, the value of lost output from shortened work lives is $80 billion per year[56]—a cost to society that rivals the medical expenses of treating smoking-induced diseases.[57]

PUFF: Fine, let's include it. But what about the *benefits* smokers derive from consuming tobacco products? Because people spend some $50 billion on tobacco each year, then the benefits of smoking for them must be valued by at least this amount.[58] That should be included on the social benefits side of the ledger.

STOP: What about the grief of premature death? The remorse, pain, and suffering that accompany a slow, agonizing demise from lung cancer? How do you propose to put a dollar value on that?

PUFF: What about the social costs in lost tobacco jobs and income from an antitobacco campaign? Even a 10 to 15 percent reduction in tobacco demand would cost some 82,000 tobacco-sector jobs, representing a payroll of $1.9 billion. Add in the inevitable ripple effects on other sectors and the job losses rise to nearly 200,000. Further incorporate the federal expenditures triggered by unemployment compensation payments and the total costs reach $5.6 billion—most of which would be disproportionately borne by southern tobacco-producing states.[59]

STOP: I think you're trivializing the issue. An economy with a gross domestic national product approaching $8 trillion—and federal government expenditures of $1.6 trillion—could easily survive the impact. And the increased consumer spending on nontobacco products and services could actually increase jobs and employment in virtually every state.[60]

But what about the ruined lives and family tragedies inflicted by tobacco consumption? The chronic illnesses and degraded quality of lives? How do you put a dollar value on those, when even discussing them in monetary terms serves to demean the human misery involved?[61]

MODERATOR: Unfortunately, although I suspect this discussion could continue interminably, our program cannot. This may be an issue where, as Sir Winston Churchill observed, the imagination is baffled by the facts.

I thank our panelists for a lively examination of social cost, public welfare, and the functioning of the market for tobacco. And I invite our viewers to return next week, when we tackle the question of the proper public policy toward the tobacco industry. Good night.

Appendix

Statement of William I. Campbell
President and Chief Executive Officer
of Philip Morris U.S.A.
before the
Subcommittee on Health and the Environment
House Energy and Commerce Committee
April 14, 1994

Mr. Chairman and distinguished Members of the Subcommittee. I am here today at your request, and I would like to take this opportunity to set the record straight on charges that have recently been made against the industry and Philip Morris. First, Philip Morris does not add nicotine to our cigarettes. Second, Philip Morris does not "manipulate" or independently "control" the level of nicotine in our products. Third, Philip Morris has not used patented processes to increase or maintain nicotine levels. Fourth, cigarette smoking is not addictive. Fifth, Philip Morris has not hidden research which says that it is. And, finally, consumers are not misled by the published nicotine deliveries as measured by the FTC method.

Mr. Chairman, I trust that you and the other Members of the Subcommittee are sincerely interested in learning the facts about the various issues raised a few weeks ago in Commissioner Kessler's presentation—issues which, I might add, are not new. The claim that cigarette smoking is addictive has been made for many years. The fact that tar and nicotine levels vary among our many products has been publicized for over 20 years. The process by which cigarettes are manufactured, and which, at our invitation, FDA representatives saw firsthand several weeks ago, has been publicly known for over 50 years. And the call for the FDA to assert, or be given, jurisdiction over cigarettes has been made and rejected by the FDA and the courts on several occasions in the past.

There were a number of incorrect statements or assumptions in Dr. Kessler's presentation. Many require a detailed rebuttal. To the

extent possible in the time available today, I will try to respond to
them and to the Subcommittee's questions.

I.   *PHILIP MORRIS DOES NOT ADD NICOTINE TO OUR CIGARETTES*

The claim that Philip Morris secretly adds nicotine during the
manufacturing process to "keep smokers addicted" is a false and
irresponsible charge. The processes used to manufacture cigarettes
have been publicly disclosed for years in patents and the published
literature. And the results of that processing—cigarettes with varying
levels of tar and nicotine reflecting varying customer preferences—
have been closely monitored and reported by the FTC, and the
manufacturers themselves in every advertisement, for 25 years.

Contrary to the claim that we are committed to maintaining, or
even increasing, nicotine delivery in our products, the fact is that
tar *and nicotine* levels have decreased dramatically over the past 40
years. Today, the market is populated with a number of "ultra low"
brands which deliver less than 5% of the tar *and nicotine* of
popular brands 20 years ago.

Philip Morris and other manufacturers have reduced delivery in
a number of ways. The most important is the use of increasingly
efficient filters which substantially *reduce* many smoke
components, including both tar *and nicotine*. Filtration reduces
nicotine delivery 35% to 45% in today's brands, as compared to a
"standard" cigarette made simply of tobacco and paper.

Through a process called ventilation, nicotine levels are
reduced by 10% to 50%. Through the use of expanded tobacco—a
process developed by Philip Morris, in which tobacco is "puffed"
much like puffed rice cereal—tar and nicotine levels are reduced
still further.

There has been a fair amount of recent discussion of the
reconstituted tobacco process. Again, that process has been thoroughly
described for years in the published literature. In that process, stems
and small leaf parts are re-formed into a paper-like sheet. The
reconstituted leaf process does *not* increase nicotine levels in tobacco

or cigarettes. *To the contrary, 20 percent to 25 percent of the nicotine in the tobacco used to make reconstituted leaf is lost and not replaced.*

These processes, when combined in the cigarettes Philip Morris sells today, *reduce* nicotine delivery levels by more than 50 percent in the case of Marlboro, to 96 percent in the case of Merit Ultima, as compared to a "standard" cigarette made of nothing but tobacco and paper.

Ignoring these reductions, some critics have focused on minute amounts of nicotine that are found in tobacco extracts and denatured alcohol—which *together* have no measurable effect on nicotine delivery of our cigarettes.

Philip Morris uses denatured alcohol to spray flavors on the tobacco. The alcohol is denatured—that is, it is made to taste bitter so that no one will drink it—*under a formula required by the BATF and found in the Federal Register.*

Again, the small amount of nicotine found in denatured alcohol and tobacco extracts cannot be measured in cigarette smoke.

The expenditure of millions of dollars to reduce tar and nicotine in these various ways undercuts any suggestion that Philip Morris is "intent" on adding nicotine to its cigarettes in an effort to "maintain" nicotine levels or to "addict" smokers.

II. *PHILIP MORRIS DOES NOT "MANIPULATE" OR INDEPENDENTLY "CONTROL" THE LEVEL OF NICOTINE IN OUR PRODUCTS*

The cigarette industry markets and advertises products by tar category to satisfy a variety of consumer preferences. Within tar categories, we attempt to provide a competitive advantage by providing the best possible taste.

When creating a cigarette for a tar category, we select a particular tobacco blend and flavors to provide "uniqueness" for the product. The most significant parameters for determining tar delivery are the amount of expanded tobacco used, filtration efficiency, and ventilation.

So, how do we "manipulate" or independently "control" nicotine as our critics charge? *The answer is we don't.* We accept the nicotine levels that result from this process.

As representatives of the FDA learned when, at our invitation, they recently visited our manufacturing center in Richmond, nicotine levels in tobacco are measured at only two points in the manufacturing process—at the stemmery, where tobacco leaves are prepared for processing, and then *18 months later* after those leaves have been manufactured into finished cigarettes. Although Philip Morris maintains over 400 quality control checkpoints in the manufacturing process—for example, moisture levels, weight, etc.—*none* measures, reports or analyzes nicotine levels in tobacco.

III. *PHILIP MORRIS HAS NOT USED PATENTED PROCESSES TO INCREASE OR MAINTAIN NICOTINE LEVELS*

Commissioner Kessler spent a great deal of his recent testimony attempting to support the proposition that Philip Morris may be using secret patented processes to increase or maintain nicotine delivery in our cigarettes. We are not.

The processes described in the patents referred to by Commissioner Kessler are not at all secret but, rather, were publicly disclosed years ago, first to the U.S. government and then to the world.

Philip Morris in fact has never used any of the processes described in these patents to increase, or even maintain, nicotine levels in any of its products. To the contrary, the only patents cited by Commissioner Kessler which Philip Morris has ever used were for the *reduction* and in some cases the virtual *elimination* of nicotine.

IV. *CIGARETTE SMOKING IS NOT ADDICTIVE*

During the March 25 hearing, Dr. Kessler and some Members of the Subcommittee contended that nicotine is an addictive drug and that, therefore, smokers are drug addicts. I object to the premise and to the conclusion.

Many people like to smoke. Some people like the look and feel of the pack or the smell of tobacco. Some like to hold and fiddle with a cigarette. And, of course, there is the taste and aroma of the tobacco, and the sight of the smoke.

Cigarettes contain nicotine because it occurs naturally in tobacco. Nicotine contributes to the taste of cigarettes and the pleasure of smoking. The presence of nicotine, however, does not make cigarettes a drug or smoking an addiction.

People can and do quit smoking. According to the 1988 Surgeon General's Report, there are over 40 million former smokers in the United States, and 90% of smokers quit on their own, without any outside help.

Further, smoking is not intoxicating. No one gets drunk from cigarettes, and no one has said that smokers cannot function normally. Smoking does not impair judgment. No one is likely to be arrested for driving under the influence of cigarettes.

In short, our customers enjoy smoking for many reasons. Smokers are not drug addicts.

V. *PHILIP MORRIS RESEARCH DOES NOT ESTABLISH THAT SMOKING IS ADDICTIVE*

At the March 25 hearing, Commissioner Kessler repeated the charges of Dr. Jack Henningfield, that in 1983, a company, later publicly identified as Philip Morris, suppressed research by one of its scientists which allegedly concluded that nicotine was an addictive substance. That claim is false.

In fact, that scientist published two full papers and five abstracts concerning the work in question *prior* to the creation of the manuscript in question. That manuscript, which was subsequently provided to the Subcommittee by Commissioner Kessler, did present some evidence that nicotine will be self-administered by rats and is, therefore, a "weak" reinforcing agent. But the manuscript itself states: "that termination of prolonged access to nicotine under conditions in which it functions as a positive reinforcer does not result in physiological dependence."

The manuscript thus did not conclude that nicotine is "addictive."

Moreover, by the time the Philip Morris researcher was ready to publish this information (1983), the "positive reinforcing" nature of nicotine had already been reported in other *published* literature. Indeed, the 1988 Surgeon General's Report states that such nicotine reinforcement was "shown conclusively" as early as *1981*, based on *government*-supported research.

VI. *CONSUMERS ARE NOT MISLED BY THE PUBLISHED NICOTINE DELIVERIES AS MEASURED BY THE FTC METHOD*

Contrary to the impression given by Commissioner Kessler that the FTC has somehow adopted a test procedure that misleads the public as to the true levels of tar and nicotine they are inhaling, the routine Analytical Smoking Methods derived from the FTC method are nearly identical to those used throughout the world to measure tar and nicotine deliveries and accurately compare brand deliveries.

All of the tests are conducted on cigarettes obtained from the marketplace. They are, therefore, the same cigarettes smoked by the consumer after all cigarette manufacturing processes have been completed.

As a result of this testing, the nicotine delivery of all commercial cigarettes is measured and disclosed to the tenth of a milligram, both in public releases by the FTC and, perhaps more importantly, *in every cigarette advertisement.*

Commissioner Kessler suggested that the FTC figures were misleading because smokers might "compensate" for lower tar and lower nicotine brands by smoking those cigarettes differently. In fact, the data indicates that, despite the dramatic reductions in tar and nicotine levels over the past decades, the number of cigarettes smoked by an individual has remained constant, and even declined slightly. More importantly, the data shows no difference in the number of cigarettes smoked by those who favor higher and lower yield brands.

Mr. Chairman, we at Philip Morris appreciate having the opportunity to respond to some of the claims made against us. We will be pleased to answer any questions you may have about these matters and to provide a more detailed written submission should that be appropriate.

Statement of David A. Kessler
Commissioner of Food and Drug Administration
before the
Subcommittee on Health and the Environment
House Energy and Commerce Committee
March 25, 1994

The cigarette industry has attempted to frame the debate on smoking as the right of each American to choose. The question we must ask is whether smokers really have that choice. Consider these facts. Two-thirds of adults who smoke say they wish they could quit. Seventeen million try to quit each year, but for every one who quits, at least nine try and fail. Three out of four adult smokers say they are addicted. By some estimates, as many as 74 to 90 percent are addicted. Eight out of 10 smokers say they wish they had never started smoking.

The issue I will address today is simple: Whose choice is actually driving the demand for cigarettes in this country? Is it a choice by consumers to continue smoking? Or is it a choice by cigarette companies to maintain addictive levels of nicotine in their cigarettes?

FDA has not regulated most tobacco products as drugs. One of the obstacles has been a legal one. The law requires an intent that the product be used either in relation to a disease or to affect the structure or function of the human body. Intent is a key word in our statute. We have not had sufficient evidence of such intent with regard to nicotine in tobacco products. The assumption has been that the nicotine in cigarettes is present solely because it is a natural and unavoidable component of tobacco.

That assumption needs to be re-examined. The amount of nicotine in a cigarette may be there by design. Cigarette companies must answer the question, what is the real intent of this design? In my testimony this morning, I will describe some of the information that has prompted our re-examination.

First, I want to address the addictive nature of nicotine. Second, I will talk in some detail about the apparent ability of cigarette companies to control nicotine levels in cigarettes.

My first point is that the nicotine delivered by tobacco products is highly addictive. As the chart shows, that fact is acknowledged by the world's preeminent medical organizations. As with any addictive substance, some people can break their addiction, but I suspect that everyone in this country has seen a friend or relative struggle to extricate himself or herself from a dependence on cigarettes and the nicotine they contain.

Remarkably, we see that nicotine exerts its grip even on patients for whom the dangers of smoking could not be starker. After surgery for lung cancer, almost half of the smokers resume smoking. Even when a smoker has his or her larynx removed, 40 percent try smoking again.

I am equally struck by the statistics about our young people. Seven out of 10 teenage smokers say they believe that they are already dependent on cigarettes. About 4 out of 10 high school seniors who smoke have tried to quit and failed. Most adult smokers today began smoking as teenagers.

It is fair to argue that a decision to start smoking may be a matter of choice. But once people start smoking regularly, most in effect are deprived of the choice to stop smoking. My concern is that the choice that people make at a young age quickly becomes little or no choice at all and it will be very difficult to reverse over the course of their lives.

The primary criteria of addictive substances are compulsive use, a psychoactive effect; that is a direct chemical effect in the brain, and reinforcing behavior that conditions continued use.

Nicotine reaches the brain within seconds. This contributes greatly to its reinforcing effect. Nicotine meets all the criteria for an addictive substance. We have learned a great deal about addictive drugs by studying laboratory animals. It is intriguing that with very few exceptions, animals will press levers and do other things to give themselves those drugs that are considered highly addictive in humans, but will not generally self-administer nonaddictive drugs. . . .

Tobacco industry officials have denied that nicotine is addictive. They use euphemisms – satisfaction, impact, strength to describe the effects of nicotine. But one company states in a quote, "It also has been generally recognized that the smoker's perception of "strength" of the cigarette is directly related to the amount of nicotine contained in the cigarette smoke during each puff."

Euphemisms aside, smokers crave nicotine pure and simple because of its psychoactive effects and its drug dependence qualities. Mr. Chairman, nicotine levels in a cigarette are more than sufficient to create and sustain addiction in the vast majority of smokers.

Let me turn to my second point today, which involves the control of nicotine levels exercised by the tobacco industry. I do not have all the facts or all the answers today. Certainly practices differ within the industry and the technology available to one company may not be available to another. It is important to keep this in mind. But a picture is beginning to emerge.

The public may think of cigarettes as no more than blended tobacco rolled in paper. But they are more than that. Some of today's cigarettes may in fact qualify as high technology nicotine delivery systems that deliver nicotine in quantities sufficient to create and to sustain addiction in the vast majority of individuals who smoke regularly.

But you don't have to take it from me. Just listen to the words written by a supervisor of research at one of the Nation's largest tobacco companies in 1972. And I quote, "Think of the cigarette pack as a storage container for a day's supply of nicotine. Think of the cigarette as a dispenser for a dose unit of nicotine. Think of a puff of smoke as the vehicle for nicotine. Smoke is beyond question the most optimized vehicle of nicotine and the cigarette the most optimized dispenser of smoke."

How does the cigarette industry design cigarettes? Several decades ago, the industry began to recognize that nicotine is the psychoactive ingredient in tobacco smoke. Numerous patents since then illustrate how the industry has worked hard to sustain the psychoactive affects of nicotine in cigarettes. . . .

Patents not only describe a specific invention but they can do much more. They speak to the industry's capabilities and research and they provide insight into what industry may be attempting to achieve with its products. . . . The number and pattern of these patents leave little doubt that the cigarette industry has developed enormously sophisticated methods for manipulating nicotine levels in cigarettes.

Look at the industry's own words in these patents. Let me read the key words from a number of patents. The industry is interested in "maintaining the nicotine content at a sufficiently high level to provide the desired physiological activity, taste, and odor."

These are the words of the patents. "Add nicotine." "Maintaining or increasing the nicotine content." "The release in controlled amounts of nicotine." "Nicotine released in controlled amounts." "Manipulation of the nicotine." "Provide various nicotine levels." "Varying levels of endogenous and exogenous nicotine." "Maintenance of the proper amount of nicotine." "Delivers a larger amount of nicotine." "Nicotine donor." "A process for the migration of nicotine." "Nicotine can be incorporated." "Nicotine-enhanced smoking device." "The application of nicotine components." "Incorporated within the filler material applied to the wrapper, applied within the glue line of the wrapper.". . .

These patents illustrate that the cigarette industry has developed technologies that allow it to add or subtract nicotine from tobacco. The amount of nicotine present in cigarettes may therefore be a matter of choice, not chance.

That prompts me to ask: How does the industry determine nicotine levels in various products? More importantly, why does the amount of nicotine in cigarettes remain in addictive levels? In fact, since the technology apparently exists to remove nicotine from cigarettes to insignificant levels, why does the industry keep nicotine in cigarettes at all?

The cigarette industry would like you to believe that it simply returns the nicotine that is removed when reconstituted tobacco is produced. It should be clear from what I have described that the technology that the industry may have available goes beyond such efforts. . . .

Nicotine levels may be dictated in part by marketing strategies and demographics. Let me show you a reproduced copy of one smokeless tobacco company's marketing strategy. The products with the lower nicotine yield [are] marketed as "starter" products. Through advertising, the users are encouraged to "graduate"—their word, not mine—to products with higher levels of nicotine, marketing on the basis of nicotine delivery.

Why develop such a strategy? The cigarette industry may tell you that the purpose of nicotine is to provide flavor. Information suggests otherwise. A company's own book on flavoring tobacco lists about a thousand flavorants, but nicotine is not one of them. Some industry patents specifically distinguish nicotine from flavorants.

As we saw earlier, technologies have been developed specifically to mask the unacceptably harsh and irritating flavor of added nicotine. In fact, U.S. patent 4,620,554 uses the word "hazardous" to describe the taste of nicotine. . . .

Why is nicotine in cigarettes? The research undertaken by the cigarette industry is more and more resembling drug development. I mentioned earlier the focus on controlling the pH of tobacco smoke because it affects absorption of nicotine. The cigarette industry has also studied the activity of added nicotine versus nicotine that occurs naturally and it has studied the potentially beneficial effects of nicotine on anxiety, heart rate, and behavioral performance tasks. Such research on the physiological effects of an active ingredient is a standard part of drug development.

Perhaps the most striking research undertaken by the industry is the quest for new nicotine-like chemicals with pharmacological properties that, and I quote from a patent, "are intended for utility as potential psychotherapeutic agents." The chart shows one patent that summarizes the effect of nicotine-like chemicals on tranquilization, sedation, and body tone of mammals.

I would like to move on to the actual nicotine levels in cigarettes. FDA laboratories measured the amount of nicotine in several types of cigarettes. We analyzed three varieties of one brand; for example, highest, medium, and lowest. What surprised us was that the lowest one in fact had the highest concentration of nicotine in the cigarettes. Let me repeat that. The lowest one in fact had the highest concentration of nicotine in the cigarette.

I have read with interest the testimony [of] Mr. Spears, Vice Chairman of Lorillard Tobacco Company. He states that, and I assume he is speaking for the industry, we do not set nicotine levels for particular brands of cigarettes. He goes on to say that nicotine levels follow the tar levels.

The easy proof, according to Mr. Spears, is that both tar and nicotine on a sales weighted basis have decreased in the same fashion and in the same amount over the years. One question: If there is no manipulation of nicotine going on, why does the lowest yield cigarette have the highest percentage of nicotine in it? If Mr. Spears is right, wouldn't the lowest yield cigarette have the lowest concentration of nicotine in it?

Furthermore, Mr. Spears says that the fact that tar and nicotine have decreased in parallel fashion over this time period, and I quote, "by the same amount" indicates that there has been no manipulation of nicotine levels. But when you look closely at the numbers from FTC's database for tar and nicotine levels in smoke since 1982, the earliest year for which the FTC-computed database is available, we do not see that kind of tar and nicotine content occurring in a parallel fashion and by a proportional amount over the last decade. . . .

We feel these data call into question Mr. Spear's conclusion and require further explanation.

The evidence I have presented today suggests that cigarette makers may intend the obvious, that most smokers buy cigarettes to satisfy their nicotine addiction. . . .

Intent is a key issue. It should be clear, however, that in determining intent, what cigarette manufacturers say can be less important than what they do. The fact that the technology is available to reduce the nicotine to less than addictive levels is relevant in determining manufacturer's intent.

Clearly, the possibility of FDA exerting jurisdiction over cigarettes raises many broader social issues for Congress to contemplate. It could lead to the possible removal of nicotine-containing cigarettes from the market, the limiting of the amount of nicotine in cigarettes to levels that are not addictive, or restricting access to them, unless the industry could show that nicotine-containing cigarettes are safe and effective.

If nicotine were removed precipitously, millions of Americans would experience addiction withdrawal. Of course, a black market in cigarettes could develop.

On these issues we seek guidance from the Congress. . . .

REFERENCES

[1] U.S. Congress. House. Subcommittee on Health and the Environment. *Regulation of Tobacco Products, part 1: Hearing Before the Subcommittee on Health and the Environment,* 103d Cong., 2d sess., 1995, pp. 72, 75 (statement of Dr. David A. Kessler, commissioner, Food and Drug Administration).

[2] W. Kip Viscusi, *Smoking: Making the Risky Decision* (New York: Oxford University Press, 1992), p. 120.

[3] Jane G. Gravelle and Dennis Zimmerman, "Cigarette Taxes to Fund Health Care Reform: An Economic Analysis," *Congressional Research Service,* Report for Congress, March 8, 1994, pp. 19–21.

[4] House Health Subcommittee, *Regulation of Tobacco Products, part 1,* p. 76.

[5] Ibid., p. 359 (testimony of R. J. Reynolds Tobacco Company).

[6] State of Minnesota v. Philip Morris, Inc., V. J. DeNoble, "Critique of 'Why People Smoke'," Mar. 16, 1983 (Trial Exhibit No. 2536).

[7] House Subcommittee, *Regulation of Tobacco Products, part 1,* p. 579 (statement of R. J. Reynolds Tobacco Company).

[8] U.S. Department of Health and Human Services, *The Health Consequences of Smoking: Nicotine Addiction, Report of the Surgeon General,* (Washington, DC: GPO, 1988), pp. 248–49.

[9] U.S. Department of Health, Education, and Welfare, Public Health Service, *Smoking and Health: Report of the Advisory Committee to the Surgeon General,* (Washington, DC: GPO, 1964), p. 350.

[10] Ibid., p. 351.

[11] House Subcommittee, *Regulation of Tobacco Products, part 1,* p. 384 (statement of Dr. Stephen M. Raffle).

[12] Ibid., p. 554 (statement of William I. Campbell, president and chief executive officer, Philip Morris U.S.A.)

[13] State of Minnesota v. Philip Morris, Inc., Claude E. Teague, Jr., R. J. Reynolds, Research Planning Memorandum on the Nature of the Tobacco Business and the Crucial Role of Nicotine Therein, Apr. 14, 1972 (Trial Exhibit No. 12,408).

[14] House Subcommittee, *Regulation of Tobacco Products, part 1,* pp. 80–91.

[15] Ibid., p. 364 (statement of R. J. Reynolds Co.).

[16] Ibid., pp. 383, 388 (Raffle statement).

[17] Ibid., p. 361 (R. J. Reynolds Co. statement). For an extensive survey, see U.S. Department of Health and Human Services, Public Health Service, Office on Smoking and Health, *The Health Benefits of Smoking Cessation: A Report of the Surgeon General,* (Washington, DC: 1990).

[18] House Subcommittee, *Regulation of Tobacco Products, part 1,* pp. 542–840.

[19] U.S. Congress. House. Committee on Commerce. *Hearing on the Proposed Tobacco Settlement,* Jan. 29, 1998 (statement of Geoffrey C. Bible, chairman and chief executive officer, Philip Morris Companies).

[20] Ibid.

[21] U.S. Congress. House. Committee on Ways and Means. *Hearings on Financing Provisions of the Administration's Health Security Act and Other Health Care Reform Proposals,* 103d Cong., 1st sess., 1994, pp. 339–40 (statement of Prof. Dwight Lee).

[22] Centers for Disease Control and Prevention, "Exposure to Secondhand Smoke Widespread" (Washington, DC: GPO, April 1996).

[23] Hearings: *Regulation of Tobacco Products, part 2,* p. 363 (statement of R. J. Reynolds Tobacco Co.).

[24] U.S. Congress. House. Subcommittee on Health and the Environment. *Hearing on Environmental Tobacco Smoke, part 2,* 103d Cong., 2d sess., 1994, p. 295 (statement of Dr. Randolph D. Smoak, Trustee, American Medical Association).

[25] Ibid., pp. 418, 422.

[26] See U.S. Congress. House. Subcommittee on Specialty Crops and Natural Resources. *Hearing on the U.S. Environmental Protection Agency's Tobacco and Smoke Study,* 103d Cong., 1st sess., 1993, pp. 67–73 (testimony of Alvin R. Feinstein, Yale School of Medicine), 147–54 (statement of Dr. Gio Gori, Health Policy Center), 155–66 (statement of Maurice Levois, Environmental Health Resources). See also "EPA and Environmental Tobacco Smoke: Science or Politics?" submission by Cong. Thomas J. Bliley (R-VA), in U.S. Congress. House. Subcommittee on Health and the Environment. *Environmental Tobacco Smoke, Hearing Before the Subcommittee on Health and the Environment.* 103d Cong., 1st sess., 1993, pp. 4–71.

[27] House Committee, *Environmental Tobacco Smoke, part 2,* pp. 425–28.

[28] C. Stephen Redhead and Richard E. Rowberg, "Environmental Tobacco Smoke and Lung Cancer Risk," *Congressional Research Service,* Nov. 14, 1995, p. 2.

[29] Ibid., pp. 53–57.

[30] See "Smokescreens," *The Economist,* Mar. 14, 1998, pp. 91–92.

[31] Flue-Cured Tobacco Cooperative Stabilization Corp. v. U.S. Environmental Protection Administration, Middle District, North Carolina, July 17, 1998.

[32] Bliley, "EPA and Environmental Tobacco Smoke," p. 71.

[33] House Specialty Crops Subcommittee, *Environmental Protection Agency's Tobacco and Smoke Study,* pp. 181–86 (statement of W. Gary Flamm).

[34] "Smokescreens," *The Economist,* Mar. 14, 1998, p. 91.

[35] See U.S. Department of Health and Human Services, *Public Health Service, Office on Smoking and Health, The Health Consequences of Involuntary Smoking: A Report of the Surgeon General,* chapter 2 (1986).

[36] National Research Council, *Environmental Tobacco Smoke: Measuring Exposures and Assessing Health Effects* (Washington, D.C.: National Academy Press, 1986).

[37] International Agency for Research on Cancer, *Monograph on the Evaluation of the Carcinogenic Risk of Chemical to Man,* vol. 38, *Tobacco Smoke,* 1986 (Lyon, France: World Health Organization).

[38] Action on Smoking and Health, "Involuntary Smoking: The Factual Basis for Action," *Special Report,* reprinted in House Subcommittee, *Environmental Tobacco Smoke, part 2,* pp. 352–55.

[39] Ashley H. Grant, "Jury: Tobacco Companies Cleared in Death," Associated Press, Mar. 19, 1998.

[40] Redhead & Rowberg, "Environmental Tobacco Smoke," p. 16.

[41] Domingo M. Aviado, "Health Issues Relating to 'Passive' Smoking," in *Smoking and Society,* ed. Robert D. Tollison (Lexington, MA: Lexington Books, 1986), p. 135.

[42] Ashley H. Grant, "Tobacco Scientist Eats Crow Over Burger Claim," Associated Press, Mar. 14, 1998.

[43] Aviado, "Health Issues," pp. 156–57.

[44] House Committee, *Review of the U.S. Environmental Protection Agency's Tobacco and Smoke Study,* p. 72 (testimony of Dr. Alvin R. Feinstein).

[45] House Health Subcommittee, *Environmental Tobacco Smoke, part 2,* p. 315 (statement of Dr. Peter W. Carter, Coalition on Smoking or Health).

[46] Sherwin J. Feinhandler, "The Social Role of Smoking," in *Smoking and Society,* ed. Robert D. Tollison, pp. 179, 185.

[47] Centers for Disease Control and Prevention, "Medical Care Expenditures Attributable to Cigarette Smoking," *Morbidity and Mortality Weekly Report,* July 8, 1994.

[48] House Ways and Means Committee, *Financing Provisions of the Administration's Health Security Act,* pp. 274–75 (statement of Clyde Behney and Maria Hewitt, Office of Technology Assessment).

[49] U.S. Treasury Department, "The Economic Costs of Smoking in the United States and the Benefits of Comprhensive Tobacco Legislation" (Washington, DC: GPO, March 1998), p. 13.

[50] House Subcommittee, *Environmental Tobacco Smoke, part 2,* p. 22 (statement of Carol M. Browner, administrator, U.S. Environmental Protection Agency).

[51] Gravelle & Zimmerman, "Cigarette Taxes," pp. 4–5.

[52] House Ways and Means Committee, *Financing Provisions of the Administration's Health Security Act,* p. 276. See also Jan J. Berendregt et al., "The Health Costs of Smoking," 337 *New England Journal of Medicine* (1997): 1052–57.

[53] W. Kip Viscusi, "From Cash Crop to Cash Cow: How Tobacco Profits State Governments," *Regulation* (summer 1997), pp. 27–32.

[54] Robert E. McCormick, Robert Tollison, and Richard E. Wagner, "Smoking, Insurance, and Social Cost," *Regulation,* (summer 1997), p. 33. For a study finding that nonsmokers subsidize smokers in the short run, but smokers subsidize nonsmokers in the longer run due to pension effects resulting from short lifespans, see Willard G. Manning, et al., *The Costs of Poor Health Habits* (Cambridge, MA: Harvard University Press, 1991), pp. 62-85.

[55] Food and Drug Administration, "Proposed Regulations Restricting the Sale and Distribution of Cigarettes and Smokeless Tobacco Products to Protect Children and Adolescents," 60 *Federal Register,* No. 155 (August 11, 1995), pp. 413–14.

[56] Treasury Department, "Economic Costs of Smoking."

[57] Kenneth E. Warner, "Health and Economic Implications of a Tobacco-Free Society," *Journal of the American Medical Association* (October 16, 1987), pp. 2080–86.

[58] Robert D. Tollison and Richard E. Wagner, *The Economics of Smoking* (Boston: Kluwer Academic Publishers, 1992), pp. 69–71.

[59] House Committee, *Financing Provisions of the Administration's Health Security Act,* p. 343 (testimony of Professor Dwight M. Lee).

[60] See Kenneth E. Warner et al., "Employment Implications of Declining Tobacco Product Sales for the Regional Economies of the United States," *Journal of the American Medical Association* (April 24, 1996), pp. 1241–46. See also U.S. General Accounting Office, *Tobacco: Issues Surrounding a National Tobacco Settlement,* April 1998.

[61] House Committee, *Financing Provisions of the Administration's Health Security Act,* pp. 315–19 (testimony of Dr. Jeffrey E. Harris).

V. War and Peace

MODERATOR: Welcome to the concluding program in our series, *The Tobacco Wars.*

Tonight we address the explosive question of public policy toward tobacco: What should we as a country do about tobacco?

Do we need a deliberate national regulatory policy? If so, what should be its major goals? Should government aim to reduce consumption of tobacco? If so, what methods should be employed?

What about the social costs of disease, death, and medical care caused by tobacco? How should these be paid, and by whom?

And what role should the tobacco companies play in any national resolution of these issues? Is their consent and participation essential for success? Is affording them immunity from litigation the price society must pay for an effective tobacco policy?

In sum, what can we as a nation do to bring peace to this war-torn battleground?

To explore these questions we are joined tonight by three distinguished panelists: Our first guest is a state attorney general. She led the team of state negotiators that developed the pathbreaking settlement with the tobacco industry proposed in the summer of 1997.[1] Welcome.

STATE: Pleased to be with you.

MODERATOR: Given what that meat-grinder of a national Congress has done to your original settlement, it must seem like ages since you developed it.

STATE: It's certainly been an object—perhaps abject—lesson in national politics.

MODERATOR: Our second guest is a former analyst in the surgeon general's office. He is a veteran over many years of the tobacco wars, who advocates a tough, "take-no-prisoners" policy toward the tobacco industry.

CRITIC: Proudly so! Thank you for having me on the program.

MODERATOR: Our third panelist is with the Economic Freedom Foundation, a libertarian organization dedicated to the defense of free markets. His views are tough, too, but in a much different direction.

LIBERTARIAN: An eminently fair characterization. I appreciate being invited to appear tonight.

MODERATOR: All right. Because she has been most extensively involved in negotiating these issues, let me begin by asking our state attorney general what she thinks an effective public policy toward tobacco should entail.

STATE: In my opinion, a meaningful tobacco policy must have four major goals: First, it must be national in scope, and, thus, it must be undertaken by the federal government. Second, it must substantially reduce consumption of tobacco products, especially among young people. Third, it must exact compensation from the industry for the social costs—past, present, and future—caused by the sale of its products. And, fourth, consumers must be accurately informed about the true health dangers of tobacco, and aided in their efforts to quit the lethal habit.[2]

MODERATOR: And you, sir? What is your policy preference?

CRITIC: I agree with the goals she's just articulated. I disagree with her, however, on the details and specific steps that I consider essential to achieve those outcomes.

MODERATOR: We'll get into those details shortly. And you, sir? What public policy toward tobacco do you recommend?

LIBERTARIAN: In my opinion, there is no need for any government policy whatsoever. There is no crisis. There is no market failure. The market is working: People are well informed about the dangers of tobacco; their consumption of it has steadily declined for 30 years and continues to do so. In this field as elsewhere, government is typically the problem, not the solution. Efforts to "fix" the problem through government policy are bound to fail and, indeed, will create more problems than they solve.

MODERATOR: Now, before we get into the details, let me ask a broader question. As you know, there's been a tremendous amount of litigation in this field. Virtually every state has launched legal proceedings against the companies. At the same time private class action lawsuits are growing exponentially.

Won't this case-by-case litigation adequately address the tobacco problem? Won't it negate the need for any government policy?

STATE: No, for two main reasons: First, legal actions are complex, slow, expensive, and burdensome, not only for the litigants but for the judicial system generally.[3]

Second, where you've got this magnitude of litigation in process, it's obvious that the early winners will obtain massive punitive damage awards. The first victorious plaintiffs —and their attorneys—will walk away with Lear jets and palatial estates. Those farther back in line, however, may face bankrupt defendants unable to pay, no matter how deserving those plaintiffs may be. A national policy is necessary in order to avoid this inequity by insuring that *all* victims and states receive just compensation for the harm they've suffered, whether they're first or last in the litigation line.[4]

Only a single national policy offers a swift, fair and consistent means for resolving the public problems posed by tobacco, while relieving the courts of the crushing burden that tobacco litigation has created.[5]

LIBERTARIAN: I agree with her, but for a very different reason. Hundreds, if not thousands, of courts, juries, plaintiffs, and defendants reaching individual decisions about the allocation of

huge amounts of resources will produce
chaos, capriciousness, and waste on an epic
scale.

The judiciary is a component of
government. So I must repeat: government is the
problem, not the solution. My recommendation
is that we demonstrate the patience and wisdom
to permit the free market to work.

CRITIC: I disagree with both of my colleagues. I think
they do our legal system a disservice.

MODERATOR: What's the basis for your opinion?

CRITIC: As I read it, the record demonstrates that
tobacco litigation has been extremely
effective: Legal action by the state of
Mississippi led to a $3.6 billion settlement.
Litigation filed by the state of Florida
culminated in an $11.3 billion settlement. The
state of Texas obtained a $15.3 billion
settlement in its case against the industry,
while Minnesota got $6.6 billion. And the
tobacco companies have settled a class action
lawsuit filed by flight attendants seeking
compensation for the secondhand smoke they
were forced to inhale on the job.[6]

In the process, the legal system has
compelled the tobacco companies to divulge
hitherto secret and incriminating documents;
to face judgment for their misfeasance and
malfeasance; to compensate their victims; to
fund antitobacco advertising campaigns; and
to curb their lethal trade practices.

Don't misunderstand me. I support tough
antitobacco legislation at the national level,

which is effective and consistently applied across the country. But if the best our elected representatives can produce is an ineffectual, toothless, or counterproductive policy, then I much prefer the litigation route.

MODERATOR: All right, then, let's move on to the details. Reducing tobacco consumption seems to be a major goal on everyone's agenda. How do we achieve it?

STATE: In my opinion, we need a multipronged approach, encompassing three mutually reinforcing features. First, we must regulate and limit tobacco advertising and marketing. Second, we must ensure that accurate information about the health risks of tobacco consumption is disseminated. And third, we must raise the price of tobacco products in order to further force down demand.

MODERATOR: What kind of advertising and marketing limits do you have in mind?

STATE: Very extensive ones: Banning tobacco company sponsorship of all activities, including concerts and sporting events; prohibiting the use of human images and cartoon characters in the marketing of tobacco products.

MODERATOR: No more Joe Camel or Marlboro Man?

STATE: That's correct. I would also ban all outdoor advertising; prohibit efforts to glamorize tobacco consumption in any media, especially motion pictures; outlaw the distribution of nontobacco merchandise—caps, jackets, bags, and so forth—bearing the logo or selling message of tobacco products; limit tobacco advertising to adult media only; and tightly regulate retail sales of tobacco products.

In addition, stronger, more truthful warning labels must be prominently placed on packages of tobacco products and in their advertising. Examples include "Cigarettes *Are* Addictive," "Cigarettes *Cause* Fatal Lung Disease," and "Smoking *Can* Kill You."

These are the major provisions contained in the Food and Drug Administration's 1996 tobacco regulation rules.[7] They also were major components of the settlement we negotiated with the tobacco companies in 1997.[8]

MODERATOR: Regulating and limiting tobacco advertising in the manner she describes seems very tough.

LIBERTARIAN: It is—and completely counterproductive, too! Prior to 1970, when tobacco firms were free from any government advertising regulations, they feverishly competed with one another to develop and market cigarettes containing far less tar and nicotine. Their advertising campaigns directly addressed peoples' concerns about health. But once we forbade them by law from employing health claims in their marketing after 1970, we destroyed their incentive to research and develop safer products—again, an outcome opposite to that intended.[9]

CRITIC: The longstanding cartel agreements among the firms that have since surfaced suggest that something other than government regulation was primarily responsible for suppressing innovation and health advertising in the field.

One problem with the marketing restraints she describes is that they won't work if they're applied only to *manufacturers* of tobacco products.

MODERATOR: Why is that?

CRITIC: Because, as Senator Lautenberg points out, they would not prevent distributors, wholesalers, and retailers from erecting billboards or otherwise engaging in the same marketing activities as the producers. Unless they're strictly applied up and down the line, from manufacturer, to wholesaler, to distributor, to final retailer and at every point in between, such restrictions would prove ineffective.[10]

LIBERTARIAN: Let's recognize these restraints for what they really are: the rankest kind of government censorship imaginable—the state dictating to private individuals exactly what they can and cannot say.

The Freedom to Advertise Coalition—an organization of advertising and media firms—vows to challenge these restraints as an unconstitutional abridgement of freedom of speech.[11] I hope it does, and that the courts agree.[12]

STATE: Admittedly, there is a serious constitutional problem. But not if the tobacco companies *voluntarily* agree to take the steps I've enumerated. Therein lies the way out of the constitutional thicket: ~~If we can offer tobacco companies an inducement sufficient to persuade them to agree to curb their marketing activities in these ways, we avoid the freedom of speech obstacle.~~

MODERATOR: What kind of "inducement" do you think would be required?

STATE: A settlement of all government legal actions against the firms—local, state, and federal— and a prohibition of private class action lawsuits. That's what we proposed in our June 1997 settlement as the quid pro quo for an agreement by the industry to voluntarily accept these limits on its marketing activities.

LIBERTARIAN: I must say I consider that to be blackmail — the state using the threat of perpetual legal harassment as a club for bludgeoning the industry into "voluntarily" acceding to government's demands. I can't imagine a grosser abuse of political power.

CRITIC: I see I'm fighting on two fronts once again!

MODERATOR: "Conversing" on two fronts, please. Why don't you address them one at a time.

CRITIC: First, my libertarian friend is concerned about "abuse of political power." But I would point out that tobacco is an industry that has perfected the manipulation of political power into a fine art form.

Here is an industry whose political clout is legendary. Here is an industry that has spent nearly $60 million on political lobbying over the last two years; pumped $4.5 million directly into the coffers of federal candidates and national political parties in 1997; and recruited eight former members of the House and Senate in its lobbying campaign. Here is an industry that has retained the services of lobbying firms linked to former Senate Majority Leaders Bob Dole and George Mitchell, as well as former Texas Governor Ann Richards. Here is an industry that fields a political army of one tobacco lobbyist for every two and a half members of Congress![13] And here is an industry that has managed to retain as its legal representative the independent prosecutor charged with investigating the President of the United States—in one of the most stunning conflicts of interest I've ever seen.[14]

MODERATOR: It does raise eyebrows when tobacco officials drop off $100,000 in political contributions on the same day they appear to testify before Congress.[15]

CRITIC: With that kind of raw political power, it's no wonder that tobacco products—lethal as they are—have for decades been uniquely privileged as neither fish nor fowl. The government has classified the industry's products as neither "food" nor "drug." As a result, this industry, and this industry alone, has been exempt from the extensive regulations that the Food and Drug Administration applies to every other food or drug product on the American market.

LIBERTARIAN: The last time I checked, the right to petition government was also a First Amendment freedom protected by the Constitution.

MODERATOR: And the second front on which you feel compelled to "converse"?

CRITIC: My state friend says it's necessary to offer the tobacco industry immunity from prosecution as the quid pro quo for circumventing constitutional issues. She justifies immunity on the grounds of "pragmatism" and "practicality." Without it, she contends, the industry would refuse to participate in resolving the tobacco problem, and the country would remain embroiled in this costly, lethal controversy.

MODERATOR: You don't accept her argument?

CRITIC: I don't, for two reasons. First, as I've just pointed out, legal action has scored unprecedented successes in this field. To derail the litigation engine by granting tobacco firms immunity from prosecution would bail out Big Tobacco at the very time when it's on the ropes and real breakthroughs are being made.[16]

It would hand Public Health Enemy #1 a "get-out-of-jail-free" card. And it would be irresponsible—as both former FDA Administrator Kessler and former Surgeon General Koop warn—to grant immunity to an industry that has unscrupulously hooked children on nicotine while denying its own research findings about the deadly effects of tobacco.[17]

Second, the fact is we already have in place a fully functioning government agency armed with technological expertise and charged with the responsibility for regulating the production and marketing of thousands of products ingested daily by millions of Americans. It is the Food and Drug Administration, and it's been operating a long time. Moreover, it doesn't have to beg, plead, or barter with an industry for permission to regulate its products, marketing, and advertising! It is constitutionally empowered to enforce its legislative mandate to protect American consumers when, where, and in the manner it considers most appropriate.

In fact, in 1996, after declaring tobacco products "drugs" and "nicotine delivery devices," the FDA issued 200-plus pages of rules comprehensively governing every significant aspect of the marketing of tobacco products.[18]

So the notion that we must immunize the tobacco giants in order to resolve the tobacco problem is, in my opinion, erroneous, unfounded, and profoundly unwise.[19]

STATE: U.S. District Judge William Osteen thinks otherwise. He ruled in 1997 that the FDA does *not* have the authority you describe for regulating tobacco advertising and promotion.[20]

CRITIC: For a district court located in the tobacco belt of North Carolina to rule that way is not entirely surprising. Let's see what happens now that his opinion is on appeal.

MODERATOR: So you don't consider any degree of legal immunity to be required in order to obtain the marketing restraints you seek?

CRITIC: I do not. After all, what else can the industry do?

STATE: We already know the answer. The industry can do what it did in the spring of 1998— walk away from the table and obstruct any national resolution of the problem. The result is gridlock: no policy; no resolution; and no benefit for the American people.

CRITIC: By refusing to support tobacco legislation, what option does the industry leave itself? Threatening to continue to addict and kill our children unless we give it unprecedented favors and bailouts? My libertarian friend just spoke of blackmail. That's economic terrorism!

MODERATOR: Let's move from marketing and advertising to the actual consumption side. How do we reduce tobacco consumption more directly?

STATE: The long term solution, given the addictiveness of tobacco, ultimately hinges on reducing tobacco consumption among young people.

MODERATOR: Why is that?

STATE: Because 80 to 90 percent of current adult smokers had their first cigarette prior to age 18, and more than half of them become regular smokers by that age.[21] Thus, the most effective way to significantly reduce smoking in the population over the long run is to dissuade people from getting hooked on it as teens. If we can do that, we will have gone a long way to curing the problem.

MODERATOR: So how should we do that?

STATE: Prohibiting marketing to young people in the ways we've just discussed is one very important way, because studies have found the young to be particularly susceptible to the blandishments of tobacco advertising.[22]

LIBERTARIAN: Ah, said Mr. Dooley, if it weren't for orphans and widows there'd be no boodle anywhere.

   Your proposal will only *enhance* the allure of smoking for the young. The more illegal, dangerous, and sinister you make tobacco, the more you heighten its appeal to the rebelliousness of young people.[23] The "visible fist" of government will produce an outcome the *opposite* of that which is intended.

   If you truly want to deglamorize the product and make it as unappealing as possible, perhaps you should simply decree that henceforth all cigarettes shall be sold only by the U.S. post office![24]

STATE: Raising cigarette prices is another important means for reducing consumption among adults and young people alike.

MODERATOR: Yet, as you know and as we explored on an earlier program, the demand for tobacco is highly inelastic because of the addictive nature of the product. Do you really think that an increase in price will have much effect on consumption?

STATE: ~~Yes, I do. You're right, the elasticity of demand for tobacco is low. But the important point is that it's not zero so that demand will decline in response to higher prices.~~

Suppose we take –0.4 as a consensus estimate of the elasticity of demand for cigarettes. That figure suggests that consumption will decline by 4 percent, on average, for every 10 percent increase in price. So, for example, if we were to double cigarette prices—a 100 percent increase—consumption should eventually decline by some 40 percent. That's no small amount: It's nearly one-half of total consumption.

Moreover, the elasticity of tobacco demand among young people is much greater —on the order of –1.0 or more. For this crucial population group, a 50 percent price hike should produce about a 50 percent drop in consumption—again, what I consider a very significant result.

MODERATOR: A plethora of tobacco policy proposals and draft legislative bills have emerged. What magnitude of price increases do they call for?

STATE: They vary. The Clinton administration, depending on the day and forum, advocates a price increase of either $1.10 or $1.50 per pack of cigarettes.[25] The price increases contained in Senator McCain's bill were more modest at first, beginning at 65¢ per pack in the first year, but escalating to $1.10 over a five-year period.[26] A tobacco bill introduced by Senators Graham, Chafee, and Harkin would have raised cigarette prices more quickly—$1.50 over the first two years.[27] The 1997 settlement negotiated between the states and the tobacco companies would have effectively raised cigarette prices by 60¢ to 70¢ a pack.

With cigarettes currently priced at an average of $2 per pack, these represent price increases on the order of 33 to 75 percent.

CRITIC: Woefully inadequate! The top-end figure of $1.50 is far less than what teens spend on a single movie. Young people spending hundreds of dollars for athletic shoes will hardly be deterred by an extra buck a week for smokes.[28] According to Congressional Budget Office (CBO) estimates, price hikes in the 60 percent range would produce only a 7 to 10 percentage decline in consumption over a 25-five year period. Even a $1.50 increase is estimated to induce only a 16 to 29 percent consumption drop.[29] Prices will have to be raised much more than that if consumption is to be significantly cut.

LIBERTARIAN: The CBO report he cites is very illuminating. It shows that continuation of the long-run, 3 percent per year decline in tobacco consumption will, over the next 25 years, swamp the relatively minor decreases induced by any of these legislated price increases. At the risk of sounding like a broken record, I must reiterate that the free market is working all by itself to reduce demand and resolve the problem.

My distinguished colleagues also neglect two other key considerations in their discussion of government-mandated increases in tobacco prices—and let me beat you to the punch by indicating that I'll address each separately!

MODERATOR: Be careful, or you'll make my role as moderator obsolete!

LIBERTARIAN: The first is the sheer inequity of such government-mandated price hikes. Raising tobacco prices would, like any sales tax, be highly regressive. It will hit lower income groups the hardest because they consume a proportionately greater share of their smaller incomes than the wealthy.

According to the Tax Foundation, 60 percent of the cost of increased tobacco prices would be paid by families in the bottom half of the income distribution—those earning less than $35,000 annually. As Paul Gigot points out, it is unconscionable to force two-smoker households to pay an extra thousand dollars a year to protect kids whose habit might harm them in 40 years, but who need food and clothes today.[30]

CRITIC: I don't see how permitting tobacco companies to destroy a low-income families' health and earning power puts any more food on their table.

MODERATOR: What's the second important consideration you think your colleagues have neglected?

LIBERTARIAN: ~~The one certain, predictable, and incontrovertible outcome of government-dictated price increases will be the emergence of a black market.~~

This is not a matter of idle theoretical conjecture. All we have to do is look at the record: California, Maryland, Michigan, and New York boost their cigarette taxes, prices rise, and what happens? Rampant cigarette smuggling—from lower-tax neighboring states, from military bases, even from Indian reservations![31] Consumption doesn't fall. But crime certainly rises.

STATE: The existence of those kinds of state-by-state differences are exactly why I maintain that a *national* tobacco policy is required—one that uniformly imposes the same price increases on tobacco products across all 50 states. That's how we avoid the black market problem.

LIBERTARIAN: Not quite. You see, an *international* black market problem still remains. Look at Canada's recent experience. As part of a "get tough" tobacco program, the Canadian government raised cigarette taxes so as to increase prices to consumers from $2.64 to $5.65 per pack over the 1983–94 period.

What was the result? Massive volumes of cigarettes were exported tax-free to the United States, where they were bought by organized crime groups and smuggled back into Canada. According to the General Accounting Office, black market cigarettes came to account for as much as 60 percent of total sales in some regions.[32]

MODERATOR: What did the Canadian government do?

LIBERTARIAN: The only thing it could do: admit the program was a failure! The black market induced by high taxes and prices had negated government control over the distribution of tobacco and undermined its objective of reducing consumption, particularly among young people. So how did Prime Minister Chrétien solve the problem? By *cutting* cigarette taxes![33]

CRITIC: The tobacco companies themselves may have directly engaged in that smuggling activity in order to subvert a policy that they opposed from the outset. The record shows that a Brown & Williamson Company executive pleaded guilty to engaging in those smuggling operations.[34] Deputy Treasury Secretary Summers has testified that substantial black market activity is not possible without the complicity of the manufacturers.[35]

STATE: The black market problem is why I remind antitobacco groups that the basis for judging an effective tobacco policy should *not* be simply to ask which one raises prices the most. Instead, it should be which one raises price to a level sufficient to significantly reduce consumption, especially among more price-sensitive teens, but not so high as to be counterproductive in the way he describes.

MODERATOR: And are you met with effusions of gratitude for making that point?

STATE: No, I'm attacked for "selling out" to Big Tobacco!

MODERATOR: Would the emergence of a black market for tobacco products have other undesirable consequences?

LIBERTARIAN: Yes. In addition to encouraging disrespect for law generally, a black market, obviously, would be completely unregulated. It thus might well offer tobacco products that are far more nicotine-laden, addictive, and dangerous to people's health than the products currently available—once again, an outcome exactly opposite to what the proponents of these policies intend to achieve. And, of course, you would have little control over underage access to this vast underground market.

On the brighter side, however, it would certainly keep Alcohol, Tobacco and Firearms agents busy running roadblocks on highways and shopping mall parking lots.

STATE: I think our libertarian colleague exaggerates the magnitude of the black market problem. As Graphic 5-1 shows, American tobacco taxes currently are among the lowest in the world. There's plenty of room to raise prices in the American market without triggering a flood of illegal imports from abroad.

However, I agree that marketing restrictions and price increases alone are not sufficient to do the job.

MODERATOR: What additional steps do you think are needed?

GRAPHIC 5-1

CIGARETTE TAXES: SELECTED COUNTRIES
1996

Country	Tax per Pack	Retail Price per Pack
South Africa	$0.47	$1.04
Taiwan	0.62	1.45
United States	0.66	1.90
Thailand	0.89	1.58
Brazil	1.06	1.43
Singapore	1.87	3.72
Netherlands	1.94	2.66
Canada	1.93	3.00
France	2.61	3.47
New Zealand	2.76	4.17
Finland	3.48	4.54
Denmark	4.02	4.75
Britain	4.30	5.27
Norway	5.23	7.05

Tax and price per pack of 20 cigarettes.
Source: Washington Post, May 16, 1998, p. A20.

STATE: We must address youth consumption even more directly by mandating specific percentage reductions in underage tobacco consumption over a period of years and by financially penalizing producers if they fail to meet those targets and deadlines.

     In our 1997 settlement, we specified that underage tobacco consumption must decline nationally by 30 percent at the end of the fifth year; by at least 50 percent by the seventh year; and by at least 60 percent by the tenth year following implementation.[36]

Legislation proposed by others more recently contains benchmarks similar to these, give or take a few percentage points.

MODERATOR: What would the penalties be if the tobacco companies failed to achieve those targeted reductions?

STATE: I think a "surcharge" of $80 million should be imposed on the industry for each percentage point by which it falls short of achieving the targeted reduction.

MODERATOR: How do you arrive at that particular figure?

STATE: It's an approximation of what I estimate as the present value of the profits obtained by the companies from underage sales.[37]

CRITIC: In principle, I endorse the concept of using targeted reductions in order to insure progress toward our ultimate goal. But the benchmarks she suggests are far too timid.

Underage tobacco consumption is illegal, period. So reduction of consumption to any level short of zero is unacceptable. And the penalties for the companies' failure to operate in accordance with the law should be much stiffer.

Moreover, most of the legislation that has been introduced is, in my opinion, fatally flawed by incorporating "caps" and limits on the amounts the tobacco companies must pay in any year. Congressman Waxman points out, for example, that Senator McCain's bill would have capped company payments at $3.5 billion per year—an amount equivalent to less than 15¢ per pack of cigarettes. That provides no deterrence. Given the huge profits involved, the companies would treat it as a small cost of doing business.[38]

Other policy proposals—including the original settlement agreement negotiated by our state colleague—permit tobacco firms to deduct their payments for tax purposes. So American taxpayers—not tobacco companies —end up footing the bill!

My position is straightforward and uncompromising: no caps; no limits; and no deductibility for tax purposes. If we're going to eradicate this sickness we have to hit the companies hard—in their pocketbooks, where they'll feel our pain!

MODERATOR: Let's turn to the issue of social costs. Tobacco, we've learned, is claimed to impose social costs on all of us—whether we consume it or not—primarily in the form of billions of dollars of medical care and expenses.

How should a national policy address this aspect of the problem?

STATE: I believe that the $368 billion figure we negotiated with the tobacco companies in the summer of 1997 does the job. Paid over a 25-year period, that amount would cover health care costs, while funding an array of research, education, and smoking cessation programs at the federal, state, and local level.

In addition, requiring the companies to "pass through" those fees to consumers would compel them to raise their prices between 60¢ and 70¢ per cigarette pack, thereby additionally contributing to our consumption reduction goal.[39]

MODERATOR: A third of a trillion dollars. Surely that must satisfy even our most skeptical critic.

CRITIC: No, I'm afraid it doesn't.

MODERATOR: But surely you must admit it's an immense amount.

CRITIC: Not when we put it in context: First, it represents only one-quarter of the amount the industry agreed to pay the state of Florida if the latter amount is extrapolated to a national level.[40]

Second, considered on an annual basis, the $368 billion amounts to $10 billion to 15 billion per year—barely enough to cover tobacco-attributable Medicare costs—with not a dime more for past damages or penalties.[41]

Third, if the payments are tied to the companies' annual sales, and if their sales decline as intended, then nowhere near $368 billion would be paid. According to the Congressional Budget Office, reasonable assumptions generate future industry payments of as little as $160 billion—less than half the $368 billion figure she cites.[42]

Fourth, the fine print of most policy proposals limit responsibility for these payments to "entities selling into the domestic market." Now, just what "entities" are these? Only the *subsidiaries* of the tobacco giants. The parent firms are not liable, nor are their extensive nontobacco or international operations. A financial check reveals the combined assets of these "entities" to be $33 billion—one-tenth the $368 billion figure and less than the payments called for over the first few years of the policies being debated. In other words, the parent firms whose assets are sufficient to make the payments escape liability, while the subsidiaries whose assets are insufficient are solely responsible.[43]

MODERATOR: You're a tough customer.

CRITIC: I'm a staunch believer in individual responsibility! The tobacco industry created this mess. The industry has profited fabulously from it. So the tobacco industry should pay to clean it up. And the payments must match the social costs. Even the McCain bill called for total long-run payments of some $500 billion,[44] while the Graham-Chafee-Harkin bill called for more than $630 billion in industry reparations.[45]

But—and this is crucial—there must be no loopholes, no tax deductions, no caps, and no exceptions or other escape hatches. So long as these loopholes are present, the spectacular dollar amounts are meaningless.

STATE: The inconvenient fact is that tobacco company funds are not infinite. Sure, we can dream up bigger sums: Why not *t*rillions of dollars rather than billions? Why not all of it paid tomorrow rather than over 25 years? But all that would do is throw the industry into bankruptcy, tie up everything in bankruptcy proceedings for decades, and "nobody gets any money."[46]

The fact is that, like it or not, we must not kill the goose that lays the golden eggs. The paramount challenge is to arrive at a payment schedule that is large enough to cover the social costs *and* that is financially feasible for the firms to fund.

MODERATOR: She makes what seems a persuasive point. Demand too much and the tobacco companies simply declare bankruptcy like Johns-Manville Corp. did in the case of asbestos, A. H. Robins Company did in the case of its Dalkon Shield intrauterine device, and Dow-Corning did as a result of its silicon breast implants.

CRITIC: The specter of bankruptcy is an empty scare tactic. In fact, forcing tobacco firms into bankruptcy might actually be good public policy.[47]

MODERATOR: Now that's a twist! How could bankrupting the industry possibly be desirable?

CRITIC: The bankruptcy laws require firms to reorganize their operations so as to emerge from the proceedings on a sound financial footing. So courts presiding over bankruptcy proceedings for tobacco firms might order them to implement the behavioral limits and restrictions we've been discussing in order to minimize their future legal liabilities and put them on a sounder financial basis. In fact, bankruptcy courts might impose stiffer behavioral restraints than those that have been proposed so far.[48]

LIBERTARIAN: Forcing the tobacco industry to shut down, of course, would be a dream come true for antismokers. It would achieve what I suspect is the ultimate goal lurking behind their other policy proposals—absolute prohibition.

MODERATOR: You've been admirably restrained the last few minutes. What's your assessment of a policy requiring the tobacco companies to pay hundreds of billions of dollars?

LIBERTARIAN: First, it's an unconstitutional denial of due process—an illegal bill of attainder that imposes criminal penalties in the absence of a trial.[49]

Second, it betrays those policies for what they really are: a massive redistribution of resources into the grasp of greedy politicians and special interest groups.

We've heard about $368 billion, $500 billion, $600 billion. Just where will that money go?

MODERATOR: I suspect you have an idea.

LIBERTARIAN: So do you. It will go to aggrandize the budgets and bureaucracies of the burgeoning antismoking lobby and its myriad allies in government. There is already a cottage industry of these special interest groups— "rent seekers," economists call them—lured by the prospect of ballooning budgets, personnel, and political influence. According to one estimate, as many as 17 new federal bureaucracies may be created.[50]

Others join the pork-fest derby: Democrats want to spend a large part of those billions on reducing class sizes in elementary schools, better teacher training, school modernization, subsidized medical care for children, and expanded child care services.[51] Republicans are considering using tobacco funds to pay for tax credits and cuts, and—to shore up their reelection prospects—to provide health care for millions of Americans.[52]

Tobacco farmers demand their piece of the pie, as do "tobacco-dependent regions"— and their representatives in Washington aim to see that they get it as their price for supporting any national policy.[53] Minority lawmakers are demanding their own special share of any settlement.[54] An "Asbestos Alliance" is demanding billions as its "rightful" share of any national tobacco deal.[55] And the National Association of Convenience Stores, and the Tobacco Vending Machine Committee, have staked their claims.[56]

Meanwhile, states are fighting Washington over the division of the spoils,[57] while individuals are suing Blue Cross plans for a share of the billions.

MODERATOR: House Speaker Newt Gingrich calls it a "big tax, big spending, big government" boondoggle.

LIBERTARIAN: In my opinion, he's right. And, of course, let's not forget the lawyers: In Florida alone, their bill comes to a cool $2.8 billion—an average of $200 million per attorney involved, or about $14,000 an hour assuming each worked 24-hours a day.[58]

When this immense amount of government money is up for grabs, the alleged "social problem" that instigated it becomes incidental. This kind of money, William Safire says, is even more addictive than nicotine.[59]

MODERATOR: But isn't that an unavoidable by-product of the political logrolling and compromise inherent in the democratic resolution of major social problems?

LIBERTARIAN: The problem is that we don't need any government policy! The free market is solving the problem effectively without the need for this wasteful rent-seeking extravaganza.

In the absence of government regulations, private firms have a strong profit incentive to provide the kind of smoking environment that people prefer. If a majority of customers prefer to smoke, a profit-maximizing firm will allow them to do it. If customers overwhelmingly prefer a smoke-free environment, then profit-maximizing firms will provide smoke-free environments.

Likewise, on the employment side private firms will also provide the type of smoking environment most preferred by their employees. If they don't, the labor market will force them to pay their workers more and to suffer higher production costs and lower productivity as a result.

In either event, the market will punish private firms for failing to resolve the tobacco problem in the most efficient way.[60]

MODERATOR: If that's true, then government regulation is either superfluous or inefficient.

LIBERTARIAN: Of course it is! If government forces firms to do what they would do on their own, then regulation is superfluous and wasteful. On the other hand, if government regulation forces firms to do something other than what they're already doing on their own, then it's counterproductive and costly.

Either way, it's wasteful.

MODERATOR: In general, then, how would you sum up your overall position on tobacco policy?

LIBERTARIAN: Forget the courts. Forget government regulation. Trust the market. It works: The risks of smoking have been extraordinarily well publicized for a half century. People have been inundated by a constant barrage of adverse information concerning the dangers of smoking. They know the risks. They know the health consequences. And they are acting on the basis of that knowledge by steadily and substantially reducing their tobacco consumption.

The market isn't perfect. It doesn't work instantaneously. It simply takes time.

MODERATOR: But in Keynes's famous phrase, in the long run we're all dead.

LIBERTARIAN: The alternatives advocated here tonight are, for me, far more frightening.

MODERATOR: In what way?

LIBERTARIAN: Think about the implications of my colleagues' arguments: If adults can't be expected to make responsible decisions about tobacco products without government protection, how can they possibly be expected to make reasonable decisions about nutrition? About matrimony? About child rearing? Or about occupational choice? Indeed, how can democracy itself be expected to function if people are considered such poor judges of their own well-being and that of others?

Conversely, if government interferes with the free exercise of voluntary choice by adults in the case of smoking, what's to stop the state from imposing similar restrictions on political expression, religious beliefs, and any of the other liberties we cherish as a free people?[61]

CRITIC: I find it supremely ironic for him to wrap his antigovernment jeremiad in the cloak of civil liberty and freedom.

MODERATOR: Why does that strike you as ironic?

CRITIC: Because he's making *my* case!

MODERATOR: In what way?

CRITIC: The tough policy I advocate has the ultimate goal of enabling people to live longer, so they can more fully enjoy the liberties he describes but which tobacco-induced death and disease deny them.

MODERATOR: Since our time is running out, let me ask our state official for her reaction.

STATE: It's an old refrain. Every effort by democratic governments to genuinely promote people's welfare has been met with fulminations about the collapse of civilization, the scourge of totalitarianism, the end of the world as we know it, and so on.

    The fact is that the "free" market my libertarian friend swoons about is not free in any meaningful sense. It's free for only a handful of tobacco giants: free for those merchants of death to addict people and their children; free for them to deceive, mislead, and confuse people about the true health dangers of tobacco; free for them to profit by commercially exploiting the drug addicts they create; and free for them to avoid responsibility for the billion-dollar burden of social costs they leave for the rest of us to pay.

    A workable tobacco policy won't be perfect or ideal. It inevitably will necessitate compromises among diverse and antagonistic interests. It won't satisfy those at either extreme end of the political spectrum. As the old cliche has it, politics is the art of the possible. The libertarian do-nothing approach merely sanctions an immensely costly enslavement to a lethal habit. Ironically, it's the same result that our critic's extremist demands will produce by precluding any reasonable resolution of the problem.

I subscribe to the Mencken dictum: "It is the dull man who is always sure, and the sure man who is always dull."

MODERATOR: Liberation or enslavement? Government oppression or private tyranny? Freedom to choose or freedom from harm? Compromise or sellout? War or peace?

These are the questions you, our viewers, will have to ponder as the tobacco saga continues to unfold.

We thank our panelists this evening. And we thank you out there for faithfully tuning in these past weeks.

On behalf of us all, good night.

REFERENCES

1 For one in-depth account of these negotiations, see Carrick Mollenkamp et al., *The People vs. Big Tobacco* (Princeton, NJ: Bloomberg Press, 1998).
2 See U.S. Congress. Senate. Committee on Labor and Human Resources. *Hearings on the Public Health Aspects of the Tobacco Settlement,* 105th Cong., 1st sess., 1997, pp. 57–61 (statement of Christine O. Gregoire, attorney general, state of Washington).
3 *Proposed Settlement Between State Attorneys General and the Tobacco Industry,* June 1997, p. 4.
4 U.S. Congress. House. Committee on Judiciary. *Hearing on Civil Liability Provisions of the National Tobacco Settlement,* 105th Cong., 2d sess., Feb 5, 1998 (testimony of Gale Norton, Attorney General, State of Colorado).
5 Proposed Settlement, p. 4.
6 U.S. Congress. House. Committee on the Judiciary. *Hearing on Civil Liability Provisions,* Feb. 5, 1998 (testimony of Professor Richard A. Daynard).
7 U.S. Department of Health and Human Services, Food and Drug Administration, "Final Rule: Regulations Restricting the Sale and Distribution of Cigarettes and Smokeless Tobacco to Protect Children and Adolescents," 61 *Federal Register* 44, 396 (Aug. 28, 1996).
8 *Proposed Settlement;* Food and Drug Administration, "Final Rule."
9 John E. Calfee, *Cigarette Advertising, Health Information and Regulation Before 1970,* Federal Trade Commission, Working Paper No. 134, Dec. 1985.
10 Senator Frank Lautenberg, "Don't Start Negotiating with Tobacco 'Terrorists'," *Roll Call,* Mar. 23, 1998.
11 U.S. Congress. Senate. Committee on Commerce, Science and Transportation. *Hearings on the Tobacco Settlement,* Mar. 3, 1998 (testimony of David Versfelt).
12 See Central Hudson v. Public Service Commission, 447 U.S. 557 (1980) for the Supreme Court's ruling with regard to government restriction of commercial speech.
13 Public Citizen, "Burning Down the House: Big Tobacco's 1997 Congressional Lobbying," March 1998; Jill Abramson, "Tobacco Industry Donating to Politicians at Record Rate," *New York Times,* Mar. 8, 1998, p. 1.
14 Robert Dreyfuss, "Double Dipper," *New Republic,* Mar. 23, 1998, pp. 10–11.
15 Jonathan D. Salant, "Tobacco Companies Give to House GOP," Associated Press, Apr. 1998.
16 House Committee, *National Tobacco Policy,* (testimony of Hubert H. Humphrey III, attorney general, state of Minnesota, Feb. 5, 1998), Senator Kent Conrad (D-ND), Address to the National Association of Counties, Mar. 6, 1998.
17 Letter from C. Everett Koop and David A. Kessler, co-chairs, Advisory Committee on Tobacco Policy and Public Health, to House Speaker Newt Gingrich and Senate Majority Leader Trent Lott, Feb. 17, 1998.

[18] U.S. Department of Health and Human Services, "Final Rule," 61 *Federal Register* 44, 396 (Aug. 28, 1996).

[19] House Committee, *National Tobacco Policy* (testimony of Professor Richard A. Daynard, Feb. 5, 1998).

[20] Coyne Beahm v. FDA, Memorandum Opinion, Judge William L. Osteen, U.S. District Court for the Middle District of North Carolina, Apr. 25, 1997.

[21] U.S. Department of Health and Human Services, Food and Drug Administration, "Proposed Rule: Regulations Restricting the Sale and Distribution of Cigarettes and Smokeless Tobacco to Protect Children and Adolescents", 60 *Federal Register* 41, 314 (Aug. 11, 1995).

[22] See the extensive evidence and sources cited in ibid.

[23] Holman W. Jenkins, "Let My Shareholders Go," *The Wall Street Journal,* Apr. 15, 1998, p. A23.

[24] Jeremy Bulow and Daniel P. Kessler, "Robbing Smokers to Pay Lawyers," *The Wall Street Journal,* Apr. 7, 1998, p. A18.

[25] U.S. Congress. Senate. Committee on Commerce, Science, and Transportation. *Hearings on Constitutional, Bankruptcy, and Tobacco Price Issues,* 105th Cong., 2d sess., Mar. 24, 1998 (testimony of Lawrence H. Summers, advocating price increase of $1.50); Lawrence L. Knuttson, "Gore: Tobacco Plan Would Save Lives," Associated Press, Mar. 22, 1998 (advocating price increase of $1.10).

[26] Jeffrey Taylor, "Senate Panel Unveils Parts of Tobacco Bill," *The Wall Street Journal,* Mar. 30, 1998, p. A3.

[27] "Summary: Kids Deserve Freedom From Tobacco Act of 1998," News Release, Senator John Chafee, Mar. 12, 1998.

[28] David Greising, "Is Big Tobacco's Antismoking Push A Smokescreen?" *Business Week,* Mar. 30, 1998, p. 40; Holman W. Jenkins, "Let My Shareholders Go," *The Wall Street Journal,* Apr. 15, 1998, p. A23.

[29] Congressional Budget Office, *The Proposed Tobacco Settlement: Issues from a Federal Perspective,* April 1998.

[30] Paul A. Gigot, "Pols Prove as Greedy as Big Tobacco," *The Wall Street Journal,* Apr. 10, 1998, p. A10.

[31] Robert A. Levy, "The Tobacco Deal: Myths and Misconceptions," *The Freeman,* Jan. 1998, p. 19.

[32] U.S. General Accounting Office, *Cigarette Smuggling: Interstate and U.S.-Canadian Experience* (Washington, DC: GPO, Dec. 9, 1997).

[33] Ibid.

[34] Ron Scherer, "Paving a Bootleg Tobacco Road?" *Christian Science Monitor,* Apr. 21, 1998.

[35] David E. Rosenbaum, "Smoking Foes Battle the Industry's Specter of Smuggling," *New York Times,* May 5, 1998, p. A24.

[36] Proposed Settlement, p. 24.

[37] Proposed Settlement, p. 53.

[38] Congressman Henry Waxman, "Preliminary Analysis of problems with the McCain Draft," Mar. 29, 1998 (draft).

[39] Proposed Settlement, pp. 34–38.

[40] House Committee, *National Tobacco Policy* (testimony of Professor Richard A. Daynard, Feb. 5, 1998).

[41] Ibid. (testimony of Hubert H. Humphrey III, attorney general, state of Minnesota, Feb. 5, 1998).

[42] Congressional Budget Office, *The Proposed Tobacco Settlement: Issues from a Federal Perspective.*

[43] Lynn M. LoPucki, "Some Settlement," *Washington Post,* Jan. 20, 1998, p. A15.

[44] U.S. Congress. Senate. Committee on Commerce, *Summary of National Tobacco Policy and Youth Smoking Reduction Act,* Mar. 30, 1998.

[45] Editorial, "Blinders Hide Tobacco Deal's Flaws," *USA Today,* Mar. 19, 1998.

[46] John Hall, "McCain Says All Lose If Leaf Deal Fails," *Richmond Times-Dispatch,* Mar. 19, 1998.

[47] Brian Fox, James M. Lightwood, and Stanton A. Glantz, "A Public Health Analysis of the Proposed Resolution of the United States Tobacco Resolution," Library and Center for Knowledge Management, University of California–San Francisco, Feb. 1998.

[48] Ann Davis, "Is Chapter 11 Just an Idle Threat by Big Tobacco?" *The Wall Street Journal,* Apr. 17, 1998, p. B1.

[49] Henry Weinstein, "Tobacco Firms Threaten Assault on Cigarette Bill," *Los Angeles Times,* Apr. 4, 1998, p. A1.

[50] Scott Williams, Tobacco Industry Spokesman, Company Press Release, Apr. 10, 1998.

[51] Press Release, "Congressman Fazio Introduces 'Health Kids Act'," Mar. 11, 1998.

[52] Jeanne Cummings and Greg Hitt, "GOP Considers Tobacco Revenue to Pay for Health-Care Coverage of Uninsured," *The Wall Street Journal,* Mar. 31, 1998, p. A24.

[53] "Tobacco Country Fights Back," *The Economist,* Mar. 21, 1998, pp. 29–30; Senator Ernest Hollings, "Farmers Must Receive Their 'Fair Shake' from Deal," *Roll Call,* Mar. 23, 1998.

[54] Peter S. Canellos, "Blacks Want Cut of Tobacco Deal," *Boston Globe,* Mar. 24, 1998, p. B1.

[55] Milo Geyelin, "Asbestos Alliance Seeks $20 Billion Under Tobacco Deal in Congress," *The Wall Street Journal,* Apr. 1, 1998, p. B6.

[56] See U.S. Congress. House. Committee on Commerce. *Hearing on Views of Business Excluded from the Tobacco Settlement Negotiations,* 105th Cong., 2d sess., Feb. 25, 1998, (testimony of Mr. Terry Davis and Mr. Carl Bolch).

[57] See, for example, U.S. Congress. Senate. Committee on Commerce, Science, and Transportation. *Hearing on Tobacco Price, Retailers, and State Issues,*

105th Cong., 2d sess. Mar. 19, 1998 (statement of Raymond C. Scheppach, executive director, National Governors' Association); and Jeffrey Taylor, "States Urge House Republicans to Keep Tobacco Dollars From Federal Coffers," *The Wall Street Journal,* Dec. 9, 1997, p. A24.

[58] Matthew Scully, "Will Lawyers' Greed Sink the Tobacco Settlement?" *The Wall Street Journal,* Feb. 10, 1998, p. A18.

[59] William Safire, "The Syntax of Sin Tax," *New York Times,* Apr. 13, 1998, p. A27.

[60] William F. Shughart II and Robert D. Tollison, "Smokers versus Nonsmokers," in *Smoking and Society*, ed. Robert D. Tollison (Lexington, MA: Lexington Books, 1986), pp. 221–23.

[61] Ibid.

Epilogue

As this book goes to press (June 1998), the tobacco wars continue unabated.

On the litigation front, the landmark lawsuit jointly waged by the State of Minnesota and Minnesota Blue Cross/Blue Shield unleashed to the public—via internet postings—a flood of incriminating, highly confidential company documents. The trial and, especially, the exhibits entered into evidence, captured the nation's attention as journalists rushed to file daily, and even hourly dispatches. The Minnesota campaign was fought up to the final skirmish. It ended in an anticlimactic, out-of-court settlement, that denied a disappointed jury the opportunity to render a verdict.

Nevertheless, the wide dissemination of compromising company documents triggered an avalanche of new lawsuits—by individual plaintiffs, by labor unions, by Blue Cross/Blue Shield programs, by cities, by Indian tribes, and even by foreign governments. At last count, some 800 lawsuits were outstanding against the industry, quadruple the number two years earlier. In this high-stakes game, the industry defiantly declared its readiness to take on all comers.[1]

On the legislative front, the Senate was ensnarled in rancorous debate over tobacco legislation. Blizzards of bills—and amendments to bills—were introduced. Some afforded the tobacco companies immunity from prosecution. Some did not. Some contained "caps" limiting the aggregate monetary damages the companies could be forced to pay in any one year. Some did not. Some were addressed only to the American market; others aimed to regulate the behavior of U.S. tobacco firms around the world. Estimates of the total cost to the industry of the evolving legislation gyrated wildly, from as low as $160 billion,[2] to as high as $870 billion.[3]

One day, congressional leaders and the President would declare the situation hopeless—only to reverse course the next day and optimistically announce that a breakthrough was at hand. Senator

McCain, Republican of Arizona, decorated Vietnam War veteran and designated point man on the tobacco bill, was variously praised as a paragon of statesmanship, or pilloried as a traitor to his party and a threat to American youth.

At the beginning of the legislative imbroglio, the tobacco companies pledged their willingness to cooperate with the Congress in fashioning a sensible national policy. Subsequently, after the evolving Senate bill failed to provide them the legal immunity they considered essential, they angrily withdrew from the proceedings. They decried the proceedings as a political gold rush, and launched an eight-week, nationwide, $40 million advertising blitz to defeat the McCain bill. With Churchillian determination, they vowed to fight the pending legislation to the bitter end.

The denouement came with unceremonious abruptness when, on June 17, 1998, the Senate killed the tobacco bill on procedural grounds. Opponents charged that "McCain's Monstrosity" had spiraled out of control; that it had expanded light-years beyond the core goal of reducing youth smoking; and that it had been transmogrified into a massive tax on working-class Americans and a boon to a bloated government bureaucracy. Proponents of the bill countered with claims that the political and economic clout of Big Tobacco had prevailed over the public interest. Both sides vowed to carry on the war in their fall campaigns: Republicans portrayed defeat of the McCain bill as a victory over a budget-busting boondoggle; Democrats deplored it as proof that the Republican Party cares more about tobacco profits than the nation's children.

Some political and industry leaders suggested that radically pared-down legislation, narrowly focused on curbing youth smoking (including revocation of driving licenses for underage consumption), could quickly be introduced in the House or in the next session of Congress. The Clinton Administration hinted it might launch its own lawsuit against the tobacco companies, seeking compensation for smoking-induced federal health care expenses. The battle may have ended, but clearly the war had not. Indeed, events came full circle when state attorneys general and the tobacco companies once again resumed negotiations for a comprehensive settlement.

Meanwhile, the daily trench warfare continued: An antismoker attacked the pilot of a commercial jetliner in midflight, because smokers were allowed to light up; two smokers opened fire on mall security guards after being asked to extinguish their cigarettes; a condominium owner sued her smoking neighbors for causing the fatal bronchitis death of her dog; and a chain-smoking chimpanzee was accused of attacking a zookeeper in a Mexican water park.

How the tobacco wars will eventually play out—whether legislation will be enacted, what particular policies it might contain, how the states' legal actions will end, how the courts will rule on the FDA's authority to regulate tobacco marketing, and what the ultimate consequences of all this will be for the sale and consumption of tobacco—remains to be seen.

Regardless of these specifics, a number of broader questions beg for resolution.

First, how should the immense sums contemplated in state settlements and federal legislative proposals be apportioned? How much should the states receive? How much should be awarded to health care plans, and how much to the individual members of those plans whose premiums were inflated by tobacco-induced disease? How much should be used to underwrite health care expenses, educational programs, and smoking-cessation programs at the federal level? Is it appropriate to use substantial portions of the proceeds for purposes unrelated to tobacco and health, such as reducing government debt, cutting taxes, or decreasing class sizes in elementary schools? What about tobacco-dependent farmers and geographic regions? Do they deserve a "fair" share?

Second, does the democratic political process inevitably unleash a feeding frenzy over the spoils? Does it inflate peripheral matters to such cataclysmic proportions that they overwhelm the original purpose of the legislation? Does it almost inevitably transform what ostensibly is a public health issue into a Christmas tree package of billion-dollar goodies to benefit politically influential interest groups? Surveying the final weeks of debate over the Senate bill, the *Washington Post* was impelled to ask, "Where's the tobacco?" as the emphasis on political grandstanding seemed to overwhelm considerations of public health.

How germane were some of the amendments attached to the McCain bill? Consider the "marriage tax" amendment, for example. Are married couples entitled to special tax relief? How much? Below what income levels? Does this discriminate against gay, lesbian, and bisexual partnerships? Or consider the fight to limit attorneys' fees. What are "reasonable" legal fees in tobacco cases, prosecuted by private law firms on behalf of the states on a contingency basis: $500 an hour, $1,000, or $4,000? Do multi-billion dollar settlements paying attorneys $10,000, $30,000 or $92,000 *per hour* constitute obscene profiteering?[4] Or do they fairly compensate law firms willing to take on government cases at no expense to the taxpayers—cases in which there is no ex ante assurance of success? Obviously, such amendments were only remotely related to the central issue of smoking and health.

Third, should the Justice Department have followed through on its antitrust victory against the industry fifty years ago and taken steps to vitiate the power of the tobacco oligopoly? If a less concentrated, more competitive industry structure had been put in place a half-century earlier, would the tobacco firms have been able to sustain their alleged conspiracy over the ensuing decades? If there had been more firms and less dominance by a few, might some mavericks have compelled the rest to publicize their research findings, to develop "safer" cigarettes and to market them aggressively?

It is striking that among all the current policy proposals, not one addresses the oligopolistic structure of the tobacco industry. To the contrary, the antitrust agencies have permitted the industry to become even more concentrated in recent years by failing to challenge the oligopoly's predatory pricing campaign against Liggett in the 1980s, and by permitting British-American Tobacco Company (the world's second largest tobacco company, and parent of Brown & Williamson in the U.S. market) to acquire American Tobacco Company and eliminate it as a troublesome independent influence in the field. Is it disingenuous for antitrust officials to bemoan anticompetitive aspects of the proposed tobacco settlement, when their own decades of inaction have sanctioned an oligopoly structure that fosters, magnifies and facilitates those anticompetitive proclivities?[5]

Fourth, are not all sides in the tobacco wars tainted with an embarrassing dose of hypocrisy? Congress and the states have always had the authority to raise cigarette taxes to discourage smoking. Tax-based price hikes could have significantly begun to ameliorate the tobacco problem years ago by curbing smoking among young people. If so inclined, Congress could also have expanded the Food and Drug Administration's powers to regulate tobacco products. Perhaps the current legislative impasse is less a matter of principle than an opportunity to generate issues for political campaigns.

Similarly, the FDA, which was created shortly after the turn of the century, could have addressed the tobacco problem long ago and ended tobacco's uniquely privileged status as neither "food" nor "drug."

State and local laws prohibiting tobacco sales to minors have long been on the books. If, as Deputy Treasury Secretary Lawrence Summers has testified, tough enforcement of those laws can slash youth consumption as much as 70 percent,[6] why have states and communities not been more vigilant in enforcing them?

Where were the watchdogs of the media, as scientific findings and medical concerns about the deleterious health effects of tobacco mounted for decades? Historically, the media have fearlessly investigated government (My Lai, Watergate, Whitewater) and major corporations (Dow, Monsanto, Exxon). Yet the media traditionally have been averse to investigating tobacco (which may kill ten times more people than AIDS).[7] Did Big Tobacco's large advertising budgets buy self-censorship on the part of the media? Similarly, the American Medical Association criticized members of the Chicago Bulls for smoking victory cigars following their NBA championship. Yet, for decades, the AMA accepted tobacco advertising in its publications. In fact, the organization insisted as late as 1964 that health warnings on cigarette packs were unnecessary and stressed the importance of tobacco taxes as a source of government revenue.[8] More recently, the California AMA stands accused of logrolling with the tobacco lobby on pending legislation.[9] Were the media and the AMA duped by the industry's machinations to deceive the public about the adverse health effects of tobacco? Or did tobacco's financial support render them willing accomplices in the industry's campaign for sowing doubt about the health effects of smoking?

And where were the multitudinous critics of legal contingency fees when some states first entered into those arrangements? Why did responsible government officials not question these fees at the time the law firms were initially retained by their states? Why did they wait to speak out only *after* the legal battles had been fought and won, and only *after* billions of dollars in settlement payments were on the table?

Fifth, in a free society, just how far should the state go in attempting to alter the behavior of individual citizens? Under the doctrine of *in loco parentis*, for example, universities once upon a time enforced strict rules prohibiting the consumption of alcohol on campus: Possession of a container of beer anywhere on campus —whether full or empty, open or unopened—was a per se violation of university regulations, and resulted in automatic expulsion without any hearing or access to "due process." The concept of in loco parentis has long since been discarded as insulting and degrading. Yet binge drinking today is a major problem on college campuses. How far should university administrations go in addressing the problem, in protecting students from each other, in protecting students from themselves?

In a free society, John Stuart Mill insisted, the individual must be sovereign over his or her own body and mind: "He cannot rightfully be compelled to do or forbear because it will be better for him to do so, because it will make him happier, because, in the opinions of others, to do so would be wise, or even right."[10] Yet Mill recognized that personal freedom cannot be absolute—that the goal must be to maximize a *pattern* of freedom for society at large.

He understood that the community has a legitimate right—indeed, an obligation—to restrain individuals in order to prevent them from physically harming others, as well to protect them before they reach "the maturity of their faculties." The perennial challenge, he saw, does not concern the abstract ideal of personal freedom, but rather "the practical question, where to place the limit—how to make the fitting adjustment between individual independence and social control. . . ."[11]

So, too, are not government restraints on the marketing of tobacco products an essential exercise of the police power of the state in order to protect the health, safety, and welfare of the citizenry? Does a government ban on tobacco advertising on billboards near schools, in sports arenas, and at NASCAR events fall squarely within this duty? Does it curb commercial speech in accordance with longstanding Supreme Court precedent and interpretation? Or, instead, does it despotically destroy fundamental First Amendment freedoms of speech? Is it an act of tyranny—not only by the state, but of what Mill called "the tyranny of the prevailing opinion and feeling," and the impulse of a majority to impose "its own ideas and practices as rules of conduct on those who dissent from them; to fetter the development, and, if possible, prevent the formation of any individuality not in harmony with its ways, and compel all characters to fashion themselves upon the model of its own"?[12]

In contemplating some of these fundamental issues, the antagonists in the tobacco wars, particularly the extremists and zealots among them, might well take heed of Abraham Lincoln's counsel: "Suppose you go to war, you cannot fight always; and when, after much loss on both sides, and no gain to either, you cease fighting, the identical old questions as to terms of intercourse are again upon you."[13]

REFERENCES

[1] Barry Meier, "Tobacco Bill's Death Is Likely to Prompt Litigation Landslide," *New York Times,* June 19, 1998, p. A19.

[2] Congressional Budget Office, *The Proposed Tobacco Settlement: Issues From a Federal Perspective,* April 1998.

[3] U.S. Senate, Republican Policy Committee, May 8, 1998.

[4] See, e.g., Robert J. Samuelson, "Welfare for Lawyers," *Washington Post* (nat'l weekly ed.), June 15, 1998.

[5] Staff Report, Federal Trade Commission, *Competition and the Financial Impact of the Proposed Tobacco Industry Settlement,* Sept. 1997.

[6] U.S. Congress. Senate. Committee on Commerce, Science and Transportation, March 4, 1998.

[7] David Hanners, "Tobacco Historically Given Little Media Coverage," *St. Paul Pioneer Press,* Jan. 25, 1998.

[8] Ibid.

[9] Sabin Russell, "Confidential Papers Expose Deals of Cigarette Makers," *San Francisco Chronicle,* July 15, 1998.

[10] John Stuart Mill, *On Liberty* (London: Everyman's Library, 1972), p. 78.

[11] Ibid., p. 73.

[12] Ibid.

[13] Inaugural Address, 1861.

Index

About the Authors

Walter Adams is the Vernon F. Taylor Distinguished Professor of Economics at Trinity University in San Antonio, Texas, and past president of Michigan State University.

James W. Brock is the Bill R. Moeckel Professor of Economics and Business at Miami University in Oxford, Ohio.

Over the last fifteen years, Adams and Brock have coauthored *The Bigness Complex*, a treatise selected by *Business Week* as one of the ten best business books of 1987, as well as *Dangerous Pursuits: Mergers and Acquisitions in the Age of Wall Street* (1989). They are coeditors of *The Structure of American Industry,* which is currently in its ninth edition.

The Tobacco Wars is their third Socratic dialogue. Two previous "plays," *Antitrust Economics on Trial* (1991) and *Adam Smith Goes to Moscow* (1993) were both published by Princeton University Press.

In addition to numerous articles in professional economics and law journals, Adams and Brock have contributed a spate of op-ed articles to leading newspapers around the country. They have also appeared as expert witnesses before Congressional committees.